ESCHATOLOGY AND ETHICS

ESSAYS ON THE THEOLOGY AND ETHICS
OF THE KINGDOM OF GOD

Carl E. Braaten

AUGSBURG PUBLISHING HOUSE
MINNEAPOLIS, MINNESOTA

ESCHATOLOGY AND ETHICS

Contents

To Wolfhart Pannenberg

Preface

I am dedicating this book to my friend Wolfhart Pannenberg. Anyone who reads his way into but a few chapters will understand why. For the last decade and more Pannenberg's influence on my theology has been growing along with our friendship. I first met Pannenberg in Heidelberg in 1957 while I was engaged in writing my doctoral dissertation on Martin Kähler, particularly his idea of "the historical Jesus and the kerygmatic Christ." We had something to talk about, because Pannenberg had begun to criticize Kähler at some crucial points where I had found him relevant. We frequently discussed the relation of "the historical Jesus" (in the several meanings of that term) to Christian faith and systematic theology. By the time I was ready to publish my first book, *History and Hermeneutics,* I had become persuaded of the rightness of Pannenberg's historical approach to theology. Topics such as revelation, salvation, resurrection, promise, eschatology, and hermeneutics became subject to historical modes of analysis and interpretation.

The upgrading of the historical pole of Christian faith had the effect of placing a higher premium on the message of the historical Jesus. The kingdom of God was the central content of this message. But what did Jesus mean by the kingdom of God? In what sense was it present in him? In what sense still future? Or was it both future and present in some way? These became the operative questions. This volume of essays goes forward with the conviction that Pannenberg has redeemed the idea of the kingdom of God for effective use in contemporary theology. The purpose of this book is not to interpret Pannenberg's thought as such, although some readers may gain some insights in that respect. The controlling intention is rather to continue and enlarge the project of eschatological interpretation in theology which Pannenberg has pioneered with such inimitable intellectual force.

The subject of eschatology can be carried in numerous directions. Some people are interested in eschatology for speculative reasons—they aspire to construct a system which drives to an interpretation of the totality of reality. Others are interested in eschatology for soteriological reasons—they want to know what the future holds for their own personal salvation. Such metaphysical and existential concerns are incorporated within the scope of my interpretation of the kingdom of God. In addition, however, I am constantly promoting the relevance of eschatology for church renewal and Christian ethics. I have called this "eschatopraxis." To have an eschatology, as it is interpreted here, is to believe that the essence of things lies in their future; nothing that exists is exactly as it ought to be; everything is subject to the call for radical conversion; and all are heirs of the promise of fulfillment.

Finally, one caveat. Pannenberg may be surprised at the directions in which I am running with the eschatological perspective. Since he has not read, let alone endorsed, the viewpoints I have developed in these essays, he bears none of the responsibility for any *faux pas* the reader might discern in my writing. My emphasis on the onesided politics of the kingdom and my sense of ecological urgency, even pessimism, may all be strange to his tastes. I don't know. It is now apparent, in any case, that the so-called "theologians of hope" are not members of a school. They are all independent thinkers, with different interests and accents. They are going in different directions. Yet, there is some kind of kinship among those who take seriously the eschatological point of departure of Christian faith and re-think the meaning of Christianity today in light of it.

The unevenness of style that appears among the chapters is due to the differences in situation in which I first communicated these ideas. Like so many others, I feel compelled to communicate the gospel at many levels—as author, preacher and classroom teacher, as well as lecturer to campus audiences, pastoral conferences and theological societies. The marks of communication *viva voce* have not been effaced. I hope that what has been lost by lack of uniformity may have been won back by a livelier pace of words and ideas.

CARL E. BRAATEN

Lutheran School of Theology
Chicago, Illinois

1

The Quest for the Meaning of Eschatology

The eschatological approach in theology today is represented by a small, but hopefully not insignificant, minority of professional theologians. This viewpoint broke into the headlines in the middle sixties under the title of "theology of hope." Like every other fad it took its brief turn at being advertised as the wave of the future. Now a decade later we know that the magic spell of catchwords like "hope" and "future" has been broken. The cultural wave on which the theology of hope was allegedly riding has already crashed on the reefs of "future shock" and "law and order."

If the theology of hope was invigorated by breathing the fresh air on the new frontiers of the Kennedy era, now it finds itself gasping for breath in the polluted atmosphere of Nixon's America. We might say that the theology of hope has lost all its fair-weather friends—all those who jump in and out of each fad as it comes along.

But the time to hope in the Christian sense is not only when reasons for optimism abound in the social and political environment. There are two trends in America in relation to which the theology of hope has a special mission. The social idealism and revolutionary romanticism that we witnessed in the decade of the '60s have been shattered by profound disappointment. In the churches this is manifested by withdrawing support from social ministry, just as Nixon is cutting back funds for public welfare. In the colleges the hot passions of revolution have cooled down to a spirit of fun and games. In relation to this trend of pulling back and dropping out, the theology of hope can generate consolation to those who were genuinely disappointed and also reinforce encouragement to remain responsibly involved in spite of the dimming of prospects for a better future for mankind.

The second trend to which the theology of hope is relevant is the religious revival in the land, marked by flight from the world in the Jesus-movement and retreat into the private sphere of inner experiences in the Spirit-movement. Hence, we face two forms of escapism: first, regression from the social and political opportunities to create a better future for all mankind, and, secondly, withdrawal into the personal space of religious other-worldliness and emotionalism. The structure of the theology of hope places a "no exit" sign at both avenues of escape. This location of the role of the theology of hope will be better understood as we explain the meaning and essence of eschatology. This is particularly necessary because eschatology itself—like its twin "utopia"—is not uncommonly believed to be nothing but an escape into a world of make-believe.

Eschatology Sans Eschaton

It may sound oddly redundant to state that the unique thing in the eschatological approach is its attempt at developing an eschatological eschatology. This is to say that in other leading schools of theology which trade on the term, we find an eschatology sans eschaton. If eschatology was truly at the core of biblical religion, particularly in the message of Jesus and primitive Christianity, it can be safely said that the history of Christianity represents a progressive de-eschatologization of the contents of the Christian faith. Of course, traditional theology always saved some room for eschatology, the eschatology of the "last things" which were treated in the last chapter of dogmatics. But there it had no organic relation to soteriology, the doctrine of the way of salvation—the *ordo salutis*—all of which was based on the person and work of Christ and mediated by the word and sacraments of the church. These *loci* were fully explicated in the middle of dogmatics, so to speak, and only at the very end did the topics of eschatology come into view. Such topics became the last things to be concerned about. They were deprived of their existential relevance, being viewed chiefly as the future outcome of things that preoccupy us now.

Traditional dogmatics seemingly had an eschaton in its eschatology, but with no connection to the existential core of its soteriology. Modern theology as a whole, from Friedrich Schleiermacher to Paul Tillich, can be seen as a legitimate reaction against this splitting of eschatology and soteriology. But in the process of drawing eschatology back to the center of Christianity, it abrogated the time dimension of the future in eschatology. Pressed hard by the rising consensus of biblical scholarship, namely, that Jewish eschatology made decisive contributions to the form and contents of New Testament Christianity, theology since Albert Schweitzer and Karl Barth has worked nobly to rebuild on foundations that could be justifiably called eschatological. But again to repeat this generalization: we have been given an eschatology sans eschaton.

Albert Schweitzer's work, *The Quest of the Historical Jesus* (1906) together with Karl Barth's *Romans Commentary* (1918) should be seen as marking the beginning of the contemporary movement to rebuild theology on the foundations of eschatology. Schweitzer's own theology, however, failed to follow up the clues represented by his rediscovery of the futurist dimension in Jesus' eschatology. He did not believe it possible to base a modern theology on his own historical discoveries. As someone has said, Schweitzer did not belong to his own school of thought. Having shown that the historical Jesus is like a plant that grew up in the soil of eschatology, he went on to say that the plant only withers and dies if we try to transplant it into modern soil. The historical Jesus must be left in his own outdated eschatological soil; there is no chance for this plant to grow in our modern gardens. So Schweitzer veered off into a mysticism of the will and left for Africa.

Every theology since Schweitzer has had to take account of his discovery, to the extent it wished to lay claim to biblical support. Many a theologian, however, has proceeded by ostensibly supporting the case of eschatology, but by one operation or another has contributed to its weakening. By co-opting the language of eschatology, it has proved possible to rob it of its incriminating force and scandalizing claim. There has been a widespread feeling that modern man is incapable of sharing the basic elements of an eschatological consciousness that shaped the

worldview of Jesus and made the early Christians spring into
action.

The full story cannot be told here of how contemporary theology since Schweitzer has contributed to the process of demolish-
ing eschatology and to an iconoclasm of the images which point
to a real future. But included in such a story we would have to
report at length how Karl Barth and Paul Althaus early in their
careers interpreted eschatology as the presence of eternity in
every moment. Later they moved away from the Platonic notion
of a timeless eternity, seeking instead to valorize the time dimensions in relation to eternity. Then the kingdom of God, as in the
later Barth, may be spoken of as a post-temporal reality, and
therefore still future and a matter of hope. The problem has
been, of course, to determine whether this is only apparently so,
whether the eschatological kingdom possesses a real future. It is
possible that in the end the kingdom of God will reveal itself to
be nothing more than what it was in the beginning. It is difficult
to see how history and time have any real meaning in such a
scheme.

Another part of the story of de-eschatologizing is Rudolf
Bultmann's existentialist interpretation of the New Testament.
The eschatological future, which Bultmann acknowledges with
Schweitzer as inherent in the message of Jesus, becomes only a
decisional possibility in every existential moment. The future
images in Jewish eschatology are classified as myth and then
flattened down to the single dimension of the present tense
through his demythologizing wringer.

Bultmann and his followers assured us that demythologizing
touches only the form of eschatology. The contents are trans-
planted into an existentialist system of concepts. A more radical
proposal was bound to be made, on the grounds that form and
contents cannot be so easily separated. This is the position of
Fritz Buri, a member of the so-called Bernese school. Buri will
do everything to retain the term eschatology, but he says Bultmann did not go far enough. We must demythologize not only
the eschatological form of the gospel but also the kerygmatic
contents of eschatology. What remains of eschatology is a concern for meaning, and this is answered á la Schweitzer in terms
of an ethical residue—the will to reverence life. But here meaning is made to spin on its own axis, and no longer revolves
around the question of the eschaton—the end and goal of life.

Along this de-eschatologizing road, we are only a thin thread away from recent radical theology and its proposal to eliminate all God-language. In a negative way radical theology possessed a fine instinct. "Belief in God and belief in the end are inseparable" said Karl Heim. If you take the end-point out of eschatology, you break the back of God-language and it collapses into meaninglessness. The same holds true for the future. If the time dimension of the future has been taken out of eschatology, what sense does it make to speak about God? The future is, after all, where all of us will spend the rest of our lives, still seeking the fulfillment we presently lack and which the promises of the gospel hold out for us as the object of ultimate hope.

It would be unfair and inaccurate, however, to state that all contemporary theology took the easy road of de-eschatologizing. In fact, most theologians resisted the entire trend exemplified by Bultmann's demythologizing, Buri's dekerygmatizing and the final collapse of God-language in radical theology. C. H. Dodd and Oscar Cullmann were all the while providing other leading options in the name of eschatology. These were found to be especially attractive to various shades of conservative persuasion. But here again we are given an eschatology sans eschaton. C. H. Dodd coined the term "realized eschatology." It means that in Christ the kingdom of God which Jesus preached has fully come. Realized eschatology would be wonderful if it were true. But is it not sheer caricature to speak of the full presence of the kingdom in this world of death and damnation? Pannenberg says, "There is an irreproachable truth in the argument that this world ought to look different if there were a God or if the Messiah had come already." [1] How better to neutralize or negate eschatology than to take the eschaton out of the future and sever its relation to the renewal and fulfillment of the whole creation?

Oscar Cullmann is associated with the theology of *Heilsgeschichte*. J. Jeremias has suggested that the eschatology in this school could be called *sich realisierende Eschatologie*—eschatology in the process of realizing itself. But on closer inspection, there is no real eschatology here at all. There is a creation at the beginning of the time line, but the line has no end. Eschatology is time running on and on in endless fashion, and that is what Cullmann calls eternity. The eternal future is time without a stop.

In this very rapid sketch of leading contemporary positions, we have argued that if Schweitzer made theology pregnant with eschatology, the ensuing development in one way or another threatened it with an abortion or miscarriage. The prefix "de" applies to this development. The process of de-eschatologizing Christianity is like peeling our vegetables; they become more palatable, but the most valuable vitamins are thrown away. Or, to change the metaphor, each theological school has assured us that its operation will only touch the outer rind, but in the end it has made deep and damaging marks on the core.

Eschatology is not so much husk that can be thrown away, leaving the kernel of the gospel intact. The "de" process gives us an eschatology without an eschaton, without hope for a final fulfillment of creation. The future of the eschaton, we are sometimes told, is either something that will never happen or something that has already happened; in any case it is not really future. Now the form of eschatology is removed, now the content. We are left with an eschatology without support for the fundamental categories of "hope" and "future." No wonder that the return of these categories to prominence in theology, under the impact of Jürgen Moltmann and Wolfhart Pannenberg, took theology by surprise. But what should have been surprising is that theology could have lived so long on a diet of de-futurized eschatology, on eschatology sans eschaton.

The Renewal of Biblical Eschatology

The question then arises whether a new interpretation of eschatology is possible which achieves a synthesis of biblical eschatology and the human quest for ultimate meaning in life. The renewal of biblical eschatology depends largely on the results of the hot debate over the theme of the kingdom of God. Is the kingdom of God an other-worldly realm that is remotely future; or is it an other-worldly realm that is immediately present? That is one possible set of alternatives. Another can be phrased like this: Is the kingdom of God a this-worldly society which will come about in the future sooner or later, or is it a this-worldly possibility that confronts us right now in the sphere of present decision? Eschatological theology would absorb these alternatives in an attempt at a higher synthesis.

According to Wolfhart Pannenberg, theology must accept

Jesus' message of the kingdom of God as the basic starting point for any new formulation of the Christian faith. He says, "This resounding motif of Jesus' message—the imminent Kingdom of God—must be recovered as a key to the whole of Christian theology." [2] The kingdom of God is the eschatological future which God himself brings about as the final fulfillment of this world. This is to be thought of as the power of the future determining the destiny of everything that exists in the present and in every past age. Pannenberg builds on the exegetical thesis shared by Albert Schweitzer and Johannes Weiss which contends that the kingdom of God was understood as eschatologically future by Jesus. Although Jesus was mistaken about the imminence of the inbreaking of God's kingdom, it was precisely this eschatological expectation that gave an end-time orientation to his whole life and qualified his message throughout.

If our thinking is synthetic, we will not dismiss all the eschatological interpretations of our great theological predecessors. Dodd's insight is to be acknowledged, in so far as there is a real presence of the eschatological future kingdom in Jesus' activity. Bultmann's insight can be admitted in that the present moment of decision does possess eschatological character in face of the futurity of God's kingdom. The eschatological quality of the kingdom impinges on every existential present. Then, too, the *Heilsgeschichte* theologians rightly emphasize that the eschatological kingdom has to do with a real future, and not merely with formal existential futurity. Both aspects must be maintained—the determinative power of the eschatological kingdom upon the existential present as well as the real futurity of that kingdom, the ground and source of that power. One can have the kingdom both ways, both future and present, in an eschatological theology with an incarnational thrust. There is a proleptic presence of the future kingdom in Jesus of Nazareth and along with it the possibility of personal participation in its salvation now through proclamation and faith.

We would summarize the eschatological view of Jesus and the kingdom of God in the following theses, drawn particularly from Pannenberg's work: [3]

(1) The eschatological rule of God which Jesus preached was the power determining his whole life.

(2) Through Jesus' complete surrender of himself to the rule

of God, he is the decisive revelatory medium of God's eschato-logical kingdom.

(3) The resurrection of Jesus from the dead was the divine vindication of Jesus' ministry as the present agency of God's eschatological revelation and salvation.

(4) The real future of the eschatological kingdom does not cease to be future in relation to its real and powerful presence in Jesus' life.

(5) The presence of the future kingdom of God is explained as a proleptic presence, namely, as an anticipation of God's eschatological rule. Thus, Jesus becomes a down-payment, as it were, of the fulfillment projected by the imagination of Jewish hope, which in apocalypticism includes the destiny of all mankind and the whole cosmos.

(6) The general resurrection is still awaited and hoped for by Christians from the fulfilling end of time and reality. The glory of God and man remains in the New Testament a matter of the future, although fore-glimmerings of it have appeared already in history by the grace of God.

It is precisely such eschatological ideas which seem so problematic. Their very strangeness no doubt continues to generate the urge to modernize Christianity at the expense of its eschatology. If we could translate Christianity into a form of mysticism, metaphysics or ethics without an eschatological remainder, we would go far to recommend Christianity even to those who despise it. But we have argued that the result is the descandalization of New Testament Christianity. Theology has its own Watergate. Certain ones have entered the eschatological headquarters of Christianity and have stolen away important stuff. Present investigations are showing that the highest authorities—the leading schools of theology—are implicated in the process of de-eschatologization.

The Future in Modern Philosophy

It has been difficult for modern theology to find a conceptual world friendly to its interest in recovering the meaning of biblical eschatology. If theology has to go it alone and do all the work of recovery by itself, it suffers the fate of being "biblical"—

using biblical words and phrases—at the expense of intelligibility in modern terms. In seeking a handle on the modern world, theology has usually looked to philosophy for help. Sometimes the philosophy in question blocks out the vision of the future and causes theology to make too easy an adjustment to the status quo.

In recent times theology has been specially attracted to existentialism. This is quite natural, because existentialism is a philosophy of the self. It seeks salvation in the inner freedom of man through detachment from the world *(Entweltichlung)*. Existentialism is also future-oriented, but the future it anticipates for the self is death. Death throws its dark shadows back upon the inner self, evoking despair, anxiety, fear, pointlessness and meaninglessness. The self exists in the world—the world of other selves, in the world of society, politics and economics. We usually call this the real world. But there is nothing in it to confirm the outreach of the self for fulfillment. So what happens? The self is hurled back upon its own inner resources, there to gaze into the abyss of its own nothingness. There is no ontological basis for hope, and the future advances with the promise of annihilation. Christian theology has tried to meet this desperate situation, first by accepting the existentialist analysis of the human predicament and its reading of the real world, and then by putting Christ—the Word of God (Barth) or the kerygma (Bultmann)—into the situation as help from the outside.

Ever since Immanuel Kant's impact on philosophy, the world which theology has faced has been split in two. There is the objective world outside; this is the objectified field of modern science, which investigates nature and history as closed systems. These systems are closed because they reckon with no new inputs from the source of ultimate reality which theology speaks of as the "freedom of God." Some theologians—and unfortunately many scientists too—continue to look upon the world in Newtonian terms. The world is a fixed cosmos, running like an electric clock according to set laws. In such a world there is no breathing space for the life of the spirit, for moral freedom and religious ecstasy. But Kant assured us that there was also the subjective realm of the self; this is the interior realm of moral means and ends, embracing freedom, decision, obedience and responsibility. Theology's grateful response was: Thank God for subjectivity; it gave him a place to be in a scientific age. Theology saw a new opening for itself—for God and the gospel—in the transphenomenal dimension of subjectivity. This is most splendidly exhibited in the thought of Sören Kierkegaard, the father of modern existentialism

Kierkegaard's influence in theology can be characterized as personalistic and existentialist; the gospel is contracted to a message of individual salvation. This theology of existence, pietistic in origin, became isolated from the world, from its social and political history. The inner changes called for in the individual to attain authentic selfhood were not such as to affect the future of the world, of man and the earth. Karl Jaspers captures the mood perfectly when he speaks of "the futility of inquiries into the future." [4] Theology which became locked in an embrace with existentialism folded the biblical eschatological horizon of the future of the world as history into the existentialist horizon of futurity as a predicate of the historicity of existence. The overarching unity of individual and society was broken, and theology went over to the side of the individual. One catastrophic result was that the promises of the gospel that came through the experience of Israel in world history, yielding an eschatology with cosmic scope, were lavished on the individual as therapy for the soul's sickness unto death. The gospel became medicine for the soul weary of living in the real world, as bad as it is.

Existentialism, and theology's alliance with it, must be seen as a retreat into the self from the objective world ruled by laws of causality. Existentialism did not question whether the world was such a mechanism of determined facts and factors; it presupposed such a world and sought refuge from it. The solitary self did not hope to change the tyranny of scientific positivism and mechanistic empiricism, but only to escape into a realm of inward-reaching meaning and freedom. All Christian assertions with respect to divine revelation and historical salvation had to be made good within the dimension of subjectivity. The truth of this generalization is in no way diminished by a loud clamor about the radical objectivity of God as the one who in his total otherness breaks in from the outside into the incommensurable sphere of subjectivity. For such a statement about God is nothing more than a subjective claim and functions exclusively in terms of the logic of subjectivity. It does so by declaring itself free of any responsibility to be tested in face of methodologically controllable criteria and claims to truth. Inevitably Christian theology was to become isolated; it could even become satisfied in its seclusion, provided it could count on non-interference from other disciplines. In short, the answer of theology to a positivism of science was a positivism of its own. Dietrich Bonhoeffer coined an apt phrase for it—revelational positivism. For a while it appeared that these two sorts of positivism could co-exist in the same mind and heart. Moltmann's judgment is apropos: "Hence the result is, as for Kierkegaard, the alliance of a theoretic atheism and a believing heart." [5] The mind reads the world in atheistic terms, but the heart knows better. This is the end result of that split between objectivity and subjectivity in the philosophy of Kant.

Theology has not limited its philosophical interest to existentialism. The later work of Ludwig Wittgenstein, specifically his *Philosophical Investigations,* is currently being hailed on another front as a promising ally for theology. It is called the philosophy of ordinary language analysis. It has the unquestionable merit of advancing the philosophical discussion beyond scientific positivism. Wittgenstein himself had earlier written a major work, *Tractatus Logico-Philosophicus,* which still stands as an important tract of positivism. Theology has been able to herald the movement of thought from the *Tractatus* through the *Investigations* as a trend decidedly in its favor. Ordinary language philosophy can help theology to analyze the logic of its own language tradition.

Theology must beware lest this newer philosophy of ordinary language analysis exercise a limiting effect on the analysis of its own rich language resources. The positivistic background of this philosophy may shine through and obscure meanings implicit in the future-oriented language of Christian faith. There is a remarkable disinterest in the logic of eschatological language among the theologians who have been swayed most by Wittgensteinian philosophy. The sole exception to this generalization is, to my knowledge, the work of Robert W. Jenson, who has succeeded in applying the techniques of language analysis to the biblical story and its gospel promises.[6] Others, however, have not found the philosophical incentive to delve into language that fastens on to the future and goads the philosopher to criticize the actual present in light of the anticipations of hope. On account of its positivistic legacy, this new philosophy of language is often content to be analytic of the status quo. One critic has referred to Wittgenstein's philosophy as a "nursery for leaving the world exactly as it is." [7] Non-revolutionary theology that indulges its interest in the *status quo* and lets that guide and delimit its quest for knowledge feels comfortable playing around in this nursery.

When theology avails itself of the logical and linguistic insights of the later Wittgenstein, it would do well to proceed with some skepticism in regard to the alleged metaphysical neutrality of ordinary language philosophy. Theology that is nourished by the eschatological resources of Christianity will understand Marcuse's criticism of positivistic philosophy. In a chapter entitled, "The Triumph of Positive Thinking: One-Dimensional Philosophy," in his book *One-Dimensional Man,* Marcuse traces certain positivistic notions about reality in Wittgenstein's later thinking.

What is positivism? It is basically a passive acceptance of reality as it is; it accepts the given frame of reference, the common use of language and the usual modes of behavior. Its greatest enemy is a revolutionary philosophy of change, whose concepts are in tension with, even in contradiction to, the established world of speech and action. Analytic philosophy, whatever else it is, suits the interest of people who like the world as it is. It is a therapy to relieve the mind of concern about the great metaphysical questions about ultimate truth and reality. Thus, it removes the only possible source of transcendence from which a steady flow of critical impulses might be released into the imagination, with the possibility of its contradicting and violating the established universe of discourse. The man on the street, plain old Joe Doe, so full of common sense, yields the raw material for the language games of the analyst. Marcuse calls attention to how trivial the language under analysis can be—"blown-up atoms of language, silly scraps of speech that sound like baby talk such as 'This looks to me now like a man eating poppies.' 'He saw a robin.' 'I had a hat.' " [8] The reader of this philosophy and of the theology created after its kind, becomes bored at receiving so much clarity on such trivial subjects.

The methods of language analysis, however, are still valid, despite their possible use in the interest of confirming the philosopher or the theologian in the convictions he already has, leaving "everything as it is." [9] Eschatological theology can become more conscious of the logic of its own language through the analysis of the use of such language in the context of lived experience. Such language is taken from the storehouse of promise, prophecy, judgment and apocalypse, from a reservoir of hopes and visions, from the lips of utopians, futurists and revolutionaries. This is not to ignore the forms of language that correspond to the empirical facts of perception, to the existing state of affairs. But the goal of language analysis need not be simply clarity, the obtaining of "clear and distinct ideas," as useful as that is. Rather, in coming to know what is, we can set about to change things, so that new language will be needed to describe the result. Reality is in constant flux. We are always in the process of creating new language to keep pace with the new reality that emerges in the course of history. The pressure of the future is upon the present, calling for repentance and faith, the willingness to let go of something we cherish and to be open to what tomorrow brings. Ernst Bloch states aphoristically: "Whatever is cannot be true." Of course not, otherwise the kingdom of God in its power and glory would be fully established throughout the world.

The language of the kingdom of God is like a sharp sword. It has the power to split our perceptions in two, so that in seeing what already exists we can leap forward in imagination to perceive the fuller state which has not yet come into being. In language we can anticipate the essential truth of reality that is not yet, but that we await in hope and sighing.

Theology today must learn from its encounter with existentialism and positivism to press on to a conception of reality as a whole that overcomes the dichotomy between subjectivity and objectification. The two sides of this split universe can be overbridged only by a flexible conception of reality as history opening toward the future. It would be fatal for theology to imagine that it could survive by retreating into the sphere of subjectivity or by accommodating itself to the objectified world of "words and things." [10] The eschatological message of the Christian faith is concerned not merely with the private things of the soul; it embraces the public realities of life in the world and concern for the future of mankind. The individual does not have a history of its own, apart from the world's; his life does not have a meaning of its own, at odds with the world's. He has his own history and meaning in conjunction with the history and meaning of all creatures—the whole creation. The truth and meaning of personal history and global history are revealed only at the end, when God shall be "all in all." But already now, as Christians know and believe, that final end has appeared as a revelation in the flesh before the end, as an initial inbreaking of the end in the life story of Jesus the Christ.

The Meaning of Eschatology

There are signs of an emergent conceptual world more amenable to the meaning of eschatology. The frozen antithesis between existentialism and positivism seems to be losing its stranglehold on modern culture, giving way to surprising outbursts of interest in what is to come. Inquiries into what lies ahead are now commonly acknowledged to be of the essence of survival. Christian eschatology does not limit its interest to questions of the longest range, namely, those which cluster around the absolute future of the world and mankind. Christianity already suffers from the widespread suspicion that it keeps its hope for heaven and its activity in the world in two separate compartments. This is to forget that the universality of God's kingdom includes the totality of the created world in all its spatial and temporal dimensions. If the kingdom of God is projected into another world, what is there left for this world but to oscillate between attitudes of self-seeking opportunism or self-defeating despair? Eschatology generates an ethic to go along with it, or it fails to keep its promise of offering the unity of life and the possibility of total fulfillment.

If eschatological theology were to choose one ally which bears the closest resemblance to its own faith in a fulfilling future, it would be the religio-philosophical outlook of Pierre Teilhard de Chardin. Hope is a faith in the future, said Teilhard. Yet, Teilhard was a trained scientist, by profession a palaeontologist, a student of past origins. He believed he could read the patterns of the future in the evidence of the past. "The study of the past has revealed to me the structure of the future." [11] Although he loved our modern scientific culture, actually he was more in love with the future than with the present. He said, "The world is only interesting if you look at its future." [12] His ideal of man was *Homo progressivus;* he is "the man to whom the terrestrial future matters more than the present." [13] As a scientist he was trained to study the past, but he found repulsive "any attitude explicitly or implicitly attributing an absolute value to the backward glance." [14] In the same vein he says, "Our nostalgia for the snows of yesteryear is morbid. What has been has now no intrinsic interest. Forward!" [15] Here are words that anticipate Ernst Bloch's philosophy: "The only thing worth the trouble of finding is what has never yet existed. The only task worthy of our efforts is to construct the future." [16]

Christian theology has yet to take the full measure of Teilhard's importance for its work. But despite eventual criticism, the first thing to be said must be a word of positive appreciation. He was a man of hope, inspiring in his contemporaries a confidence in the future at a time when it was, as he said, " 'good form' to deride or mistrust anything that looks like faith in the future." [17] He had in mind the grip that existentialist pessimism held on his fellow countrymen. There lies, however, an ambiguity in Teilhard's idea of the future which detracts from its usefulness to eschatological theology. His basic idea of the future was teleological, not eschatological. His main access to thinking about the future was, in his own terms, scientific extrapolation. By studying the past he believed it possible as a scientist "to extend a curve beyond the facts, that is to say, to extrapolate." [18] The traceable evolutionary swing upwards from inorganic to organic, from prehuman to human, forms may be extended to ultra-human forms that lie in the future. "Rightly understood, the theory of evolution offers us a lesson of hope," [19] said Teilhard. But is this truly the basis of Christian hope? Is the evolutionary process, even with God out in front of it, the hope of the world and the hope of each person living now, and perhaps dying under the steam-rollers of history? Is a teleological conception of the future an adequate translation of the eschatological horizon of the future of God in the story of Jesus' life, death, and resurrection?

The eschatological and Teilhardian perspectives join in affirming a belief in an ultimate fulfillment. The final destiny of all things will not be an everlasting abortion. But there are also shades of difference. Teilhard's thinking is more optimistic in the progressive line so characteristic of the nineteenth century. In contrast, the eschatological approach stresses more discontinuity, fulfillment through negation—like resurrection through crucifixion. It stresses the negative principle, the deadlines of death and tragedy in history. There is no continuous, onward and upward sloping of things in a progressive movement toward the eschaton—the Omega Point. Actually there is real defeat, real tragedy, and real negation of human hopes in history. This perspective would emphasize more the "in spite of" character of biblical faith. In spite of human failure, in spite of present frustration, in spite of diminished prospects for a better tomorrow, the whole adventure of life is buoyed up by the promise of God to bring about a magnificent consummation of all things —on account of Christ.

Many critics have observed that Teilhard did not take seriously the dimensions of evil in experience. Perhaps we could say that he looked away from the contingent events of frustration and failure. Teilhard tended to have a great deal of confidence in teleology, a built-in purpose in the movement and direction of events. He combined with this, however, an unswerving faith in the power of the future—the God ahead of us—to draw all things unto himself. In this trust he was drawing upon the same eschatological reserves as the theologians of hope.

Wolfhart Pannenberg has made the clearest attempt to explicate the meaning of eschatology. The central notion in eschatology is the kingdom of God. Hope for the coming of God's kingdom is focused on the future of man. The kingdom of God brings such peace and righteousness which the kingdoms of this world cannot achieve by means of human rule. The human striving for peace and justice is perpetual, but always frustrated by the sinful perversion of power. Only the rule of God will bring about a truly human society. But in the present time the conditions do not exist in which the righteousness of God rules the relationships among people. A fundamental change in the conditions of human existence is required if the rule of God is to be truly manifest. Furthermore, if the righteous rule of God is to prevail, not only for future generations but for all the generations of men going back to Adam, then some event must occur to unite all mankind. This event is called "the resurrection of the dead."

The eschatological statements of the Bible often provide a happy hunting ground for sharpshooters who predict the future. Pannenberg denies to them such value. They are not predictive in character, although they seem to have the logical form of predictions. Forecasts based on biblical prophecy come true with the same degree of accuracy as would an examination of the entrails of a chicken. We cannot read our future as though it were already past. That would be to turn faith into sight and fore-sight. How then are we to interpret eschatological statements? Here is Pannenberg's most succinct definition: "The eschatological prophecies of the future formulate the conditions of the final realization of man's humanity as a consequence of the establishment of the righteousness of God, which is essential to man's being as such." [20] The goal of eschatological salvation is the final and total realization of the essential humanity of man; but this cannot be brought about by man himself. If the human condition were flawless—if there were no sin—one would have good reason to hope for the final realization of the human potential without the intervention of the power of God. We have the need for eschatological statements precisely to keep the vision of the essential future of man alive under conditions of human existence which make its realization impossible. The final realization of the human potential is not possible for an isolated individual. Each person is a member of society. Thus, there is a social dimension in the realization of the humanity of man. Ultimately, the kingdom of God envisions not only the integration of an individual into his immediate society but also the integration of all individuals—past, present and future—into the everlasting society of freedom and fulfillment, in the unity and peace of the Spirit, through the resurrection of all the dead.

Eschatological statements do not tell us *how* such a new set of conditions will come about through the course of empirical history; they do not tell us anything about the system of links between the events that run forward to the *future in history* and the apocalyptic events that signal the arrival of the final *future of history;* and they certainly do not give us anything like a clockwork agenda of last things that will usher in the end of the world. Pannenberg states, "The eschatological hope leaves such questions open." [21] One is free to enjoy his own most pleasant speculations on the matter. Pannenberg himself suggests the possibility of a contortion or curvature of time, analagous to that of space in the theory of relativity, to explain the relationship between the eschatological future of the world and the physical processes of life in which we are now involved.

The eschatological future, for Pannenberg, is identical with the eternal essence of things.[22] Does this take the real future of the kingdom into a timeless cloud of eternity? Pannenberg thinks not. The kingdom is still future in so far as the essence of things has not yet been realized. And yet, it is just this future kingdom that is the essence of things past and present. Pannenberg is groping towards a revision of the traditional understanding of essence and eternity in relation to time. He does not conceive of the essence of things as non-temporal. The essence of things depends on the temporal process and will be decided only by way of its outcome, though it has determined the identity of everything in the past. Likewise, eternity is not conceived of as non-temporal; it also is constituted by the historical process, especially by its outcome. On the other hand, time is not just a sequence of momentary events, but of events that contribute to the identity or essence of things. In every process—here Pannenberg sounds a bit like Tillich over against the Whiteheadians —there develops something, and that something is not merely an aggregate of momentary events, nor is it just a possibility. Whatever it is that is enduring in the process is called the essence of a thing. So Pannenberg will not abolish the notion of essence; but he does relate it structurally to the temporal process.

In this scheme, the final future of the temporal process will definitely decide concerning the essence of things. The future of eschatological hope will decide about the nature and destiny of man. Nothing else conceivably could. Meanwhile, the essential future is already present through anticipation, and thus it can provide identity to our personal life, although the process of our lives is still open, and we do not know what particular events the future will bring. Eternity gives the depth of mystery to the reality of the future. Man yearns not only for progress in time, but for a lasting fulfillment in eternity. A future without eternity amounts to meaningless change, and this in turn threatens our personal identity. This personal identity lives from its essence, its essential future, which participates in the mystery of eternity.

The hope for the final realization of the human potential in the unity of its personal and social dimensions has great relevance to the human quest for meaning in life. The category of meaning designates a structural aspect of all human experience. What is the meaning of meaning? It is a matter of relation between the parts and the whole. Words have meaning, but the precise meaning in question can only be found by their use in a sentence. Bernard Lonergan has illuminated this relational feature of meaning very well: "Heuristically, then, the context of the word is the sentence. The context of the sentence is the paragraph. The context of the paragraph is the chapter. The context of the chapter is the book. The context of the book is the author's *opera omnia,* his life and times, the state of the question in his day, his problems, his prospective readers, scope and aim." [23] Pannenberg performs the same operation with events as Lonergan does with words. As words in a sentence, so also events derive their meaning from their context in a life-situation. We experience events by relating them to the totality of our life, now mediated to us through recollection and expectation. Since our life is still going forward in an unfinished process, we inevitably reach ahead by anticipating the final whole of life that is not yet a reality. Meaning is thus tied to history. The whole of life is involved in the historical process. The future comes into play, especially the final future, in order to decide the meaning of life as a whole and all its individual experiences.

If the final future plays such a role in deciding the meaning of our life experiences here and now, the question of the nature of that final future becomes most crucial. There are not many possibilities from which to choose. The choice is utterly simple: either death and that is all, or death and somehow life beyond death. Our symbol of life beyond death is resurrection. Death, however, can hardly bring the fulfillment of our identity and essence. It works de-struction on the structure of life; it brings annihilation. Only the quality of life beyond death through the power of resurrection can work retroactively on the present to ground its experiences in an ultimate structure of meaning. In light of the resurrection of Jesus Christ, death becomes demoted to the rank of a penultimate eschaton of earthly existence. Apart from the resurrection unto life eternal, death would reign supreme because it would gather all things into itself as their final end. The one who wins in the end walks off with all the marbles!

A Future-oriented Method in Theology

A decade ago, hardly a Protestant theologian would have known about Father Bernard Lonergan. Yet, while approaching his seventieth birthday, he is the author of the most important recent book on theological methodology, entitled *Method in Theology*.[1] During his years of academic obscurity he taught dogmatics at the Gregorian University in Rome, in a situation he has called "hopelessly antiquated." His early works were written in Latin on the Trinity and Christology. Then, as he recounts it, Catholic students began pouring down from Germany, France, Holland and Belgium. A vital exchange ensued; these students confronted him with insights from existentialism and phenomenology, and he presented new insights taken from his major philosophical work, entitled *Insight: A Study of Human Understanding*,[2] which he had already completed before arriving in Rome. Over 700 pages of fine print, it is the sort of massive achievement on which a reputation would be as slow in coming as it could be long in lasting. For his Catholic students it was the bridge they needed from the outdated world of Thomistic scholasticism to the new world of critical philosophy and historical reflection.

After Vatican II one began to hear of Lonergan's name through the influence of a widening circle of students who had been in Rome. Many of them were bold to take positions in advance of Lonergan, but expressed deep gratitude to him for showing them the way to go. Most radical among these was Charles Davis, who has said, "I am convinced that I myself should never have been able to leave the Roman Catholic Church, had it not been for my reading of Lonergan."[3] But already it is plain that Lonergan's boosters are divided on their evaluation of his importance. There is already talk about right-wing and left-wing Lonerganians. The difference is this: the right-wingers hail Lonergan as a kind of new Aquinas, who has constructed a modern comprehensive theory of knowledge that leads back to classical theistic metaphysics. The old dogmas rest quite comfortably on these foundations. In favor of their interpretation they can point to the fact that Lonergan does not apply his intellectual skills to contest or alter any of the traditional doctrines and symbols of the Roman Church. The left-wingers, on the other hand, tend to see Lonergan more as a new Kant, who aims to give a person not so much a position to hold as a way to go. So they go wherever their own insights lead them, even if it means dropping the system they learned from Lonergan. They can quote Lonergan in their favor, for according to him he wrote *Insight* so that an individual could discover himself and "appropriate his own rational self-consciousness." [4] It is not a system to be learned as a new *summa* of truths, but an objectification of modalities of consciousness which each person can explore within himself. It is a philosophy which starts with the individual subject reflecting on his own thought processes. In this sense it is a piece of modern critical philosophy, that is, post-Kantian.

If Lonergan's thought previously languished in the remote sanctuaries of Catholic scholarship, it can now be hoped that it has been irreversibly drawn into the open forum of international discussion. In 1970 there was an International Lonergan Congress held in Florida, attracting a group of over seventy Catholic and Protestant scholars, philosophers and theologians, scientists and writers; they gathered to celebrate and discuss the thought of this great Jesuit intellectual. This was followed up by another Lonergan Congress held in Ireland, in 1972, widening the discussion to include European scholars who had not been able to attend the earlier congress. The spirit of these congresses exhibits one of Lonergan's ideals: the pure, unrestricted desire to know the truth. The eros for the truth aims to advance insight and to attack what Lonergan calls *scotoma*—blind spots that result from aberrations of understanding. Critical reason requires an uninhibited framework of freedom in order to eclipse the scotosis that is the unconscious source of "bias" and "partial viewpoints."

The Anticipatory Structure of Knowledge

Our interest in Lonergan's work is motivated by an awareness of the great need in theology to develop a clear method appropriate to its own subject matter. We believe that Lonergan's dynamic concept of knowing can be useful to a theology in which the future of ultimate reality is the supreme category of orientation. However, we shall tend to agree with Schubert Ogden's criticism of Lonergan's total achievement: "It is adjectively transcendental and substantivally Thomist." [5] He takes in the transcendental criticism of Kantian philosophy and applies it awkwardly to repristinate the timeless ontology of Thomism. The project suffers from a serious case of hernia. A dynamic account of knowing is coupled with a static concept of being.

Before we go into the specific contribution Lonergan makes to theological method, it is necessary to understand the basic elements of his theory of understanding. His book, *Insight*, is to be understood as "a campaign against the flight from understanding." [6] It aims to disclose a thorough understanding of the nature of understanding. "Thoroughly understand what it is to understand, and not only will you understand the broad lines of all there is to be understood but also you will possess a fixed base, an invariant pattern, opening upon all further developments of understanding." [7] This is not a classical rationalist philosophy of immutable ideas and principles and norms, but a modern transcendental deduction of the invariant structures immanent in the dynamic process of knowing. There is something unchanging; that is the ever-recurrent structure of rational self-consciousness that is operative in changing situations. Man is, says Lonergan, a heuristic structure, a structurally patterned dynamism whose questioning knows no limits. The basic fact of mind is its ceaseless questioning, its nisus toward the infinite. The image of God in man *(imago dei)* is his infinite potentiality to transcend every answer, to convert every answer into another question, to be unlimitedly open to the mystery of being. To be alive, Lonergan says, "is to attend continuously to the present, to learn perpetually from the past, to anticipate constantly the future." [8] Ultimate reality—we could say "eschatological reality" —would be the complete set of answers to the most complete set of questions. It involves universality, totality and finality of being.

Our question to Lonergan's theory is whether his striving for a total understanding of the process of understanding and of all that is to be understood in its totality would not be advanced significantly if he would include the theme of the future in his reflections. The question is how to thematize the future in cognitional theory and metaphysical thought. The answer to this question will have potentially far-reaching consequences for a theological method that is intent on bringing to contemporary expression the ultimate meaning of whatever it was that happened in the history of Jesus of Nazareth. In Jesus of Nazareth the kingdom of God became an incarnate reality in such a way that to be related in faith to him is to be opened to the ultimate future of a universal fulfillment for all mankind. This commitment to the eschatological self-disclosure of God in the Christ-event does not remain neutral over against one's theory of knowledge and view of the world. Rather, such a conviction offers clues to the theologian, assisting him to form a hypothesis which calls for verification with reference to relevant data. This means that reason and faith are not apart from each other, let alone against each other, but work fructifyingly upon each other in a creative way. Thus, an *intellectus quaerens fidem* is always supported by a reverse movement of *fides quaerens intellectum*. *Intellectus* without *fides* leads to shallow rationalism; *fides* without *intellectus* opens the door to mindless emotionalism.

Our persisting question is whether Lonergan's theory of knowledge reflects the eschatological dimension of Christian faith. His understanding of the nature of understanding does not take adequately into account the fore-consciousness of the future of reality, which ought to appear somewhere in his description of the polymorphic character of the human mind. We use the word "adequately," because we do acknowledge that his notion of heuristic anticipation in the knowing process is a promising idea. It implies some kind of awareness of the future of reality which is not yet fully known. However, this trend in Lonergan's thinking could be advanced still more if his concept of being would be impregnated with the dynamism of the future, and thus become even more isomorphic with his theory of the dynamic structure of knowing. The anticipatory dimension of knowing corresponds to a dimension of "not yetness" in the reality of being itself. Such an orientation in philosophy might lead to a new metaphysic which can serve to challenge and en-

courage theology to take more seriously its own eschatological
thematic, in a way that it has failed to do ever since the so-
called process of Hellenization began.

The Christian theologian ought to consider what it is that he
might seek and find in philosophy. My own view is that the
most fruitful contact with philosophy is one which serves to
drive theology more deeply into its own theme. A test that can
be applied is whether a given philosophy stimulates theology to
express its own theme under the new conditions of experience
and knowledge. The main theme of theology, as I grasp it, is
the message of the eschatological future of God that has arrived
in the history of Jesus, his cross and his resurrection to new
life. Hence, a philosophy which itself has "a bias for the future"
(E. Bloch) might be best suited to stir the theological imagination to learn deeply from its own sources and to find a new
shape under the conditions of contemporary modes of thought
and experience.

For Lonergan knowing is a dynamic structure which includes
many elements. Among these are *experience, understanding* what
one experiences, *reflection* on that understanding, and then making a *judgment*. However, is not anticipation a prior activity of
human knowing? What kind of operation is this—to anticipate?
One does not anticipate what is already known; yet, if one does
not know what he is anticipating, he will not be able to pursue
a meaningful inquiry. Lonergan does give a significant place to
the element of anticipation in the structure of knowing. Anticipations are constitutive of the heuristic structure of all knowing,
including what goes on in the fields of science and ordinary life.
This concept of the heuristic character of knowledge is an important disclosure of the very structure of human existence.
The human mind is polymorphic, as Lonergan states, but it
would not be "alive" if it were not driven by the urge to know
the as yet unknown. "The heuristic structure is immanent and
operative in all human knowing." [9]

Another way of speaking about this heuristic structure is in
terms of man's openness to the future. Lonergan does speak of
"openness" as man's pure, unrestricted desire to know. To know
what? Being! Could he also speak of this orientation in man as
openness to the future? Could he futurize the being to be known?
If he were to do this, he would move in the direction of the
school of philosophers and theologians who have thematized the

idea of the future. This would release new possibilities of thought and expression into Lonergan's system. So I would ask whether he has paid sufficient attention to the proscopic element in man's quest for knowledge, for the whole truth about reality that is not yet whole? Lonergan has given us valuable insight into insight, but how about insight into foresight—into "the knowledge of things hoped for?" [10] He has succeeded in analyzing the mind of the scientist and the philosopher, in tracing back to their foundations the sorts of operations they are accustomed to making. But how about the mind of the prophet and the poet, the story-teller and the myth-maker? In Lonergan's analysis of mind, he tips the scale in favor of the philosopher and his transcendental inquiry, as though that were the most important function of the human mind. Thus, while he recognizes that dimension of mind which reaches out to Being in so far as it is yet unknown, it is not equally clear that he grounds the logic of anticipation, exhibited in the process of inquiry, in the reality of being in so far as it is yet unfinished. Perhaps it is a too static ontology which prevents Lonergan from laying *sufficient* stress on the dynamic, open, future-oriented structure of the mind. This would result in a greater appreciation for the function of imagination and the role of myth in the knowledge of ultimate reality. Lonergan seems to hold a purely negative view of myth.[11] As long as the future of reality has yet to become actual, the mind can only represent it in linguistic images or in myths as a patterned arrangement of symbols. Lonergan has almost nothing to say about the faculty of imagination.

It is the power of imagination to construct an image of the future that can continually drive man into the open and support the self-transcending movement of human existence. It is surely proper that Lonergan should provide us with an insight into "the insights of mathematicians, scientists, and men of common sense." [12] But there is, besides this, the uncommon sense of those who go beyond the present in announcing the right and rule of the oncoming future, to shatter the present, to break its back, in order to make way for new reality. This is not a faculty of which the professional philosopher has received a rich endowment. Yet, this may well be that aspect of mind that is theologically most significant, because through it is mediated the criticism of the present (prophetic judgment) and participation in the Realm of the Future (the kingdom of God as grace and salvation). To be more specific, that power of imagination that was surely operative in Jesus of Nazareth, if we but look to the sources as critically examined, is not adequately accounted for in Lonergan's study of human understanding.

Some men, at least, are possessed by an urgent desire to "know" the future, by way of participating in a liberating power that transcends the present. The Old Testament in fact speaks of "knowing" as a kind of participation in reality that transcends the objectively existing set of facts. This faculty that some manifest to a high degree, others may succeed in ignoring altogether. However, it may be in principle an element in the so-called invariant structure of human knowing that Lonergan attempts to illuminate. Where this faculty is fully operative, man is aware that he is living in a "split" condition. He exists in a schizophrenic situation. He is "heart and soul" oriented upon a totally other dimension of reality, that is basically different from the "here and now" in which he exists. This creates a division in himself. He exists in the present, but he longs for the future. He is a citizen of two worlds, the world of the here and now, and the coming new world that stands over against him, and indeed is already now breaking in upon him, setting up a storm of unrest and revolutionary opposition in relation to the dominion of the present, its "powers and principalities." This is an idea of apocalyptic derivation, that has usually been dealt with as unworthy of the philosopher's serious attention. Like when Kant broke through to the idea of "radical evil," against the trend of the philosophy of the Enlightenment, Goethe accused him of having "shamefully defiled his philosopher's cloak with the stain of radical evil." Since Lonergan is so intent on showing continuities and coherencies, he would perhaps not welcome the stain—or better, the strain—which this apocalyptic element would introduce into the system. But it can be shown, purely phenomenologically, that when at least some men appropriate their own self-consciousness in the most accurate way, they find that their mind is split within itself, throbbing with the antithesis between knowledge of the existing state of affairs and awareness of the Realm of the New Being that is coming. I do not think that Lonergan has given due consideration to this dualistic element in the human mind, which is so important for Christian theologians who seek to think "between the times."

But it is not only Christians who exist self-consciously in the tension between the oldness of the fading present and the newness of the coming future. Most Christians in fact collapse the tension, either by immersing themselves in the *Status Quo,* or by fleeing into an imaginary *Heaven Above.* The traditional Christian theologian or philosopher has usually handled the problem by doing both at the same time. Intellectually he has taught a theology of heaven, while enjoying the benefits of the status quo. This is the wrong kind of dualism, one which, however, has been very much at home in the smooth coordination of the natural and the supernatural in traditional Thomism.

Lonergan has addressed himself to the phenomenon of conversion. Conversion is as "if one's eyes were opened and one's former world faded and fell away." [13] That sounds good in an essay on theology. But should it not be worked out in one's general theory of understanding? And if it had been, *Insight* would have become an even more useful "handmaid" of a theology whose historical sources mediate an eschatological message. Then this faculty of imagination which is a participation in the realm of the oncoming future would have been analyzed as potentially universal. It belongs to man as man, though most men may succeed in arresting its development or stifling its sensitivity. There are non-Christians who are aware of the irreconcilable conflict between the present set of facts and the realm of the future which has a greater right to be. There is a minority of creative people—the remnant of the kingdom in world history— who have an ache in their soul for an ultimate perfection, as "the Father is perfect." This longing for perfection is active in the present as the awareness of misery, hunger and exploitation, generating a rebellion against the establishment of darkness and evil. Meaningful life is not only intellectual inquiry into the depths of being, but also a practical aggressiveness against the structures of evil, based on a belief in conversion—the convertibility of things as they are. The knowledge of truth is not only focused upon what reality contains, but also on what it fails to contain. Knowledge of the deficiency of reality makes the present meaningless if it cannot be transcended, i.e., converted by a future in which the deficiency is overcome. Knowledge that is not eschatologically oriented seriously undermines the meaning structure of all existential inquiry.

This uncommon sense of being open to the counter-reality of

the future, that arrives both in judgment and grace, is a rare gift. It is a matter of inspiration; it is soul-knowledge. However, its domain is not a supernatural realm above the natural. The ecstasy of knowing that is a fore-grasp of the future is natural, however rare. It is as natural as creativity, equally rare. But both ecstasy and creativity are thoroughly human. Those who do not yet enjoy these gifts are not human enough. To reiterate, I fail to find that Lonergan's cognitional analysis has given sufficient attention to the dimension of the future in human knowing. One sign of this is virtual silence on the negativity principle in epistemology and ontology. To take this up would place us not merely in the company of mathematicians, philosophers and men of common sense, but in the company of Isaiah and Ezekiel, of Jesus and John, of Augustine and Luther, of Marx and Bloch, to name but a few whose mental operations could hardly be squeezed into the framework of *Insight*.

To illustrate what I am saying in more philosophical terms, I would point to Ernst Bloch's concept of *docta spes*. Bloch has elevated hope and its correlate the future to a place of prominence in philosophy. The task of philosophy is to teach hope as a way of thinking. Thought may be reflection on things as they are, or if it is driven by hope, it may cross beyond the boundaries of existing facts through an anticipating consciousness. Thinking may transgress the present by anticipating the future. Classical philosophy has not developed an appropriate system of concepts to express hope for the future. Philosophy has been dominated by the introspective or retrospective moods, leaving the prospective approach out of account. Knowledge since Plato has been recollective *(anamnesis)* or analytical; its proleptic or anticipatory dimension has not found its adequate place in epistemology. "Longing, expectation, and hope need their own hermeneutic, the dawning of what is before us demands its specific concept, the new *(Novum)* requires its concept of the frontier *(Frontbegriff)*." [14]

The Future as a Mode of Being Itself

Knowledge corresponds to reality. If anticipation is an integral element of the activity of knowing, is it more than that? Does it not correspond to the shape of reality itself? Anticipation is then more than a subjective mood; it is a medium which mir-

rors the motion of reality as such. Reality has not yet become
what anticipation holds for it. Here I am about to question
whether Lonergan's notion of "timeless being" [15] is really appropriate to Christian speech about God. For Lonergan being is
eternal because it is timeless. This makes it difficult to see that
what happens in time can make a difference to this eternal
being. If this is so, hardly any discussion is needed to prove that
it is a notion quite antagonistic to the biblical picture of Jahweh
who cares infinitely about what happens in time. For the care of
Jahweh is lavished upon the event of Jesus of Nazareth, who is
radically a temporal event. One could say that whatever the
philosophical liabilities of the notion of timeless being, its theological demerits are innumerable. It inhibits one from making
sense out of the biblical narrative.

An alternative to the notion of timeless being is the idea of
being with the future as fundamental to it. The future is the
fount of temporal existence. The essence of a thing is not in a
world above this world or behind this world; but it lies in its
future. The reality of matter lies in its futurity. From the future
there is disclosed the identity of meaning and being. Bloch's
idea of the "ontological priority of the future" offers an alternative to Lonergan's notion of timeless, eternal being. It is more
than an aphorism to say that "the real genesis is not at the beginning, but at the end." [16] Reality is eschatological from the
beginning, and not only from the point of view of an arbitrarily
given supernatural revelation.

The question we are posing is whether all the dynamism in
Lonergan's system is not on the side of the subject-pole, thus
building into his cognitional theory the modern commitment
to openness, whereas on the other hand, the object-pole remains
bound to the classical prejudice for an immutable, timeless
being. If being is the whole, and the whole will exist as such
only at the end, then the object of anticipation must itself be
involved in the process of movement and change. If, on the
other hand, the whole already exists in its fullness, then whatever happens in history would seem to make no difference in
the end or to the end.

It seems that Lonergan does want to rethink the idea of God
in relation to the openness of man and his world. To follow
through on this start, the idea of truth will have to undergo
revision. In our Western concept of truth we can trace out two

roots, the Hebrew and the Greek. In an essay, "What Is Truth?" Wolfhart Pannenberg has compared these two roots.[17] For the Hebrews, in contrast to the Greeks, truth is reality seen in terms of history. Truth is not something that lies hidden in the core of things; instead it is something that happens. But the two views of truth have something in common. For example, both think of truth as something dependable and lasting, and opposed to lies and surface appearances. And although the Hebraic view of truth is oriented to historical change and an open future, trust in God is based on that trustworthiness of his which has already been shown in past historical actions. This is not totally unlike the Greek confidence in the rational structure of the cosmos, whose dependability has also been experienced in the past. Nevertheless, the difference is significant. The Greeks could not bring *truth* and *change* together. The unity and wholeness of truth could only be grasped in terms of a concept of reality whose essence is unchangeableness, and therefore without inherent temporal relations. The biblical concept of truth, in sharp contrast, requires change, in fact, real conversion. Truth is not what is and always has been; it is on the way; it is what will be. So the unity of truth has to be grasped historically. Historical change is not something that lies on the level of appearance and opinion, which is where the Greeks left it. Rather, historical change can be taken up into the concept of truth, if truth itself has a history.

Reading Lonergan often recalls Hegel to mind. Lonergan acknowledges certain similarities; in particular, his idea of "higher viewpoints" and "higher integrations" parallels Hegel's *Aufhebungen*. Someone looking for a Ph.D. thesis topic could well explore Lonergan's relation to Hegel, but this would become all the more fruitful if it were done within the wider context of the current reaffirmation of Hegel. For Hegel "the true is the whole." The truth of the whole, or the whole truth, becomes manifest only at the end. The problem that arises is to maintain this accent on the eschatological character of truth without fleeing into a realm outside of history, as Hegel did, where the historically factual and the existentially personal are voided of concrete meaning. I do not think that a reaffirmation of Hegel's point is possible for us without keeping one eye on Karl Marx and the other on Sören Kierkegaard. The trialog between Hegel and Kierkegaard and Marx is still, in my opinion, a most fruitful one to pursue. The challenge is to take up their valid criticisms of Hegel into a "higher integration" in which Hegel's key point that "the true is the whole" is retained. To accomplish this, one should not think of truth as something timeless and immutable. It is bound up with the process of history in which changes occur. Then a history, so full of contradiction along the way, can be seen as a unity in light of the end, so that the meaning of any single event is derived from its relation to the final end. The problem is how to maintain the unity and wholeness of reality while it is underway, during this time of its incompleteness. The temptation is to solve the problem in the Greek way, through a concept of timeless being. There is an alternative; it is connected with the assertion that the eschatological finality of truth and reality has made a surprising appearance in mid-stream, in Jesus of Nazareth. The unity of truth can be held together with its historicity and its openness to the future on the basis of the eschatological structure of reality as history that is manifest in the arrival of the kingdom of God in the person of Jesus.

The notion of timeless being contends against the elements of futurity and newness that are deeply bound up with the Christian hope. The new reality anticipated by hope is something that never ceases to be future. It is not the case that truth is something that surfaces from the depths of being that is always the same. That would leave no room for the idea of the future and the experience of newness. Nor is it the case that the new future is only the outcome of a process of development, as though it were always indwelling things as their *entelechy*. Lonergan's idea of finalism [18] like Aristotle's idea of *entelechy* is unable to give expression to the arrival of the really new in history and experience. Philosophically the question is whether it is possible to give an adequate evaluation of contingency, newness, freedom, change, individuality, and time itself, without grounding it in an ontology in which futurity is a modality of being itself.

The idea of the ontological priority of the future is a project of thought that has been advanced by Ernst Bloch, and has been worked over into a theological conceptualization by Wolfhart Pannenberg, at least in broad terms. Here God is not thought of as timeless immanence in a changeless cosmos, but rather as the imminent future or the creative eschaton of reality in process. Futurity is not only a feature of the temporal structure of human experience; it is grounded in being itself. God is his own future, otherwise there would be some other future beyond him, and this then would have to be thought of as God. The very idea of God requires that we think of him as the ultimate future. The direct implication of this is to think of God as "pure freedom." To be wholly free is to have one's future already within oneself. In this way we can ground the theological assertion that radical dependence on God is the fullest freedom. The essence of God who is really God is the freedom which man is seeking when he is in search of the truth and reality of his own identity. I think that a doctrine of the reality of God along these lines can best develop a response to modern atheism that takes atheism's passion for freedom seriously. Modern atheism has arisen as a protest for freedom. This protest can be advanced and not thwarted if it can be shown that the freedom man lacks has its source in God. In going ahead to freedom, man is approaching freedom's source in God. The reality of God is the power of the future which opens man to new possibilities and supports him in the very act of his freedom. The notion of timeless being can not encompass these concerns for futurity, newness and freedom, which are so deeply rooted in an eschatological worldview.

The Future in Theological Method

I share the enthusiasm others have voiced over the shift in Lonergan's thought from *Insight* to *Method in Theology*. His current reflections on theological method are carried out within the horizon of historical consciousness. The concept of "horizon" is itself one of his favorites and also enjoys common usage in the hermeneutical line that runs from Heidegger through Gadamer to Pannenberg. Lonergan clearly grasps the gulf between classical consciousness and today's historical consciousness. He is at work on the issues of continuity and change. The idea of perennial philosophy, to which he seems still to cling in *Insight,* has slipped away in his later work. He is now willing to accept a disengagement from classicist thought forms and its invariant structures and instead operate on the basis of historical premises and its more vulnerable procedures.

Lonergan has set forth the basic elements of a theological

method under the chapter title "Functional Specialties" in *Method in Theology*. This description of theological method has the distinct advantage of making it more complex than it has been in the various reductionist methods of existentialist and hermeneutical theologies. But we shall show that it remains deficient by not thematizing the orientation to the future that is basic to eschatological theology.

Lonergan begins his methodological reflections by observing the fact that the field of theology has become so specialized that the scholar is driven to know more and more about less and less. The whole of theology may be said to be divisible into eight functional specialties: (1) research, (2) interpretation, (3) history, (4) dialectic, (5) foundations, (6) doctrines, (7) systematics, and (8) communications. By differentiating these functions method is being stretched out in order to provide a sufficient basis for a new comprehensive synthesis of the results of modern field specialization that characterizes theology since the Enlightenment. These eight functional specialties can be divided into two groups of four, the first dealing with theology's orientation to the past, the second with its orientation to the present. But in what way does this analysis of the operations of method in theology give expression to the horizon of the future, essential both to biblical faith and Christian life today? In discussing the theme of the future in theological method, we shall confront Lonergan's thinking with Pannenberg's idea of the horizon of the future in historical hermeneutics. First, however, it is well to have before us a clearer picture of Lonergan's functional specialties.

The first functional specialty is *research*; it makes available the data relevant for theological investigation. In principle, such data can be fed into an information-retrieval system, saving the theologian lots of time he now spends at rummaging around for the facts. He may be trying to establish the critical text of Scripture or recreate a historical period through archeological research. Second, *interpretation*: it searches for the meaning of a fact in its original historical context. This operation is commonly called hermeneutics. Here we are involved in the interpretation of a text or recovering the author's own meaning. Third, *history*: this is a critical account of the facts in their interconnectedness. History tells us who did what, where, when and under what precise circumstances. We are seeking an account of the Christian movement, its antecedents and consequents within the context of general world history. Fourth, *dialectic:* its task is to consider the conflicting and contradictory aspects in the history of the Christian tradition. If history shows us that the Christian movement has given rise to a series of oppositions, dialectic tries to understand the reason for the conflicts and diverging viewpoints from within the structure of faith. Its aim is to seek a comprehensive viewpoint today within the larger ecumenical context, rather than to stick blindly to a party line.

It is evident that these four functional specialties are oriented to the past. The theologian is a critical listener of the word in history, encountering and assimilating past traditions. But theology does not end as an inventory of the past. It has something to pass on, to take a stand toward the present situation. The remaining four functional specialties comprise this second present-oriented phase of theology. The fifth function in method is thus *foundations:* the theologian here tries to thematize the basic horizons of experience and knowledge within which it is meaningful to formulate religious doctrines. These basic horizons are intellectual, moral, religious and Christian. The theologian is an incarnate thinker, a creature of space and time. Therefore, his account of these basic horizons are concrete, personal, dynamic, communal and historic. Sixth, *doctrines:* here theology brings to expression what must be affirmed or denied on the basis of the previous operations, but always within the horizon of contemporary experience. Seventh, *systematics:* every doctrinal affirmation gives rise to further questions. There is no unquestionable statement. An effort must be made to understand the *meaning* of doctrinal and moral decisions, and to explicate them most fully within an appropriate system of conceptualization, such as, Platonic, Aristotelian, idealist, existentialist, or what have you. The aim of systematics is to reveal coherence and remove all inconsistencies within the system of doctrines set forth. Eighth is *communications:* the aim is to reach out beyond theology *per se,* in the direction of interdisciplinary relations, such as art, literature, the natural and social sciences. It latches onto cross-cultural studies; it moves into the communications media, press, TV, group process, community structures, etc.

Lonergan has given us an analysis of the basic operations of theological method; it can hardly be improved. It makes plain that no one mind can master all the fields; it warns the theologian not to leap to ultimate results before he has considered the various operational steps along the way. Such a careful division of labor is needed "to curb one-sided totalitarian ambitions." [19] Each of these specialties has its own excellence, and none of them can promise the attainment of the end of theological inquiry by itself. This method will achieve for theology what *Insight* aimed to do for philosophy—to attack every one-sidedness, partial viewpoints and blind spots.

Perhaps we should let well enough alone, and not call for any further complexifying of theological method. That would, however, disregard the time dimension of the future that is co-constitutive of the hermeneutical framework of theological inquiry. The reality of God and the meaning of Jesus Christ can be adequately expressed neither within the horizon of the past nor within the horizon of the present. Both are essential to theology, however. The horizon of the past is essential in theological understanding, for the biblical texts can be illuminated only by taking account of its own complex of questions and answers. The interpreter's present horizon must remain so flexible and open that it not eclipse the past horizon of the biblical events. The interpreter must see the gulf between the two horizons—the horizon of the past text and the present situation. It is necessary to build a hermeneutical bridge which takes into account the particularity of each horizon. If one horizon is collapsed into the other, a reductionism occurs—either modernism or fundamentalism. Either the past is forced to echo the special interests of the present (modernism), or the present is made to bear all the burdens of the past (fundamentalism). Each one is in bondage to its own self-sufficient horizon.

Interpretation cannot truly occur through a competition between the horizon of the past text and the horizon of the present situation. A third horizon may emerge to embrace them both, without negating the particularities of the two horizons that appeared strange to each other. It is at this point of how to fuse or merge the two horizons that Pannenberg moves us to consider the horizon of the future in historical hermeneutics. The two horizons can be merged only when the total context of history within which both move is projected. The total context of history—that is history which is rounded out by projecting its future horizon. The full meaning of the past is not yet available at the present time. In a sense, only the future will tell.

The meaning of a past event always lies in its future; its ultimate meaning lies in its ultimate future. As history moves on, every interpretation of the past is open to revision. Pannenberg calls the total context of history "universal history." [20] Intrinsic to the idea of universal history is the future horizon of history. The meaning of the past and the present is to be determined in the future. The final meaning of all the events in history will be disclosed only by the final future of history, in short, when history has come to an end.

The meaning of the history which the theologian interprets, calling upon all the mental operations which Lonergan analyzes, is linked to the horizon of the future. The horizon of the past can be fused with the horizon of the present through their common orientation upon the horizon of the future end of history. Thus, a serious wrestling with the historical problem in theological method opens up the question of a possible eschatological interpretation of history. Eschatology is anticipated through the quest for meaning in history. This is congruent with the historical discovery of the thoroughly eschatological character of Jesus' preaching of the kingdom of God.

Eschatology was in the center of Jesus' message. His was a message of hope and salvation for the world. Early Christianity proclaimed the eschatological message of the future of God and the coming of his kingdom in Jesus of Nazareth as the ultimate goal of human hope and the cosmic process. The more one delves into the heart of biblical eschatology, the more it opens up the horizon of the future. No one who wrestles with the contents of biblical eschatology can be satisfied to live and move exclusively within the horizons of the past-present reality. He is moved to hope for the future of man that infinitely surpasses the record of his achievements in history.

It may seem paradoxical that the Christian faith is simultaneously rooted in the past history of Jesus Christ, grounded in the present experience of the believing church, and still oriented to the future as no other religion. The paradox may be only apparent, for it is the real history of Jesus Christ that mediates the power to attract faith in him today, thus constituting the church, and also to generate anticipations of the future. The history of Jesus has such inexhaustible power because the eschatological future of God's kingdom became really present in him, giving us a vision of the shape of things to come.

3

The Making
of a Christian
Worldview

Medieval schoolmen used to illustrate the problem of free will by telling the story of Buridan's ass. Standing at an equal distance between two bales of hay, the ass died of starvation, unable to decide whether to turn right or left. Modern theology, similarly, is becoming anemic as it stands indecisively between two extremes. On the right everything is tagged by the prefix "re." "Re" stands for going back—return, restore, revive, recover, repristinate. This is also the way of conservative restorationism. On the left the terms all begin with the prefix "de." The "de" process is the style of modernist reductionism—demythologizing, desacralizing, dekerygmatizing, dehistoricizing, deeschatologizing. Whether by swallowing the past whole or by relieving itself of its content, theology finds itself in a desperately anemic condition. Theology may suffer the fate of the ass, if it cannot find a better alternative.

The theological program of Wolfhart Pannenberg provides a new alternative beyond the competing reductionisms that have fitfully appeared in the headlines in recent decades. Measured by Bernard Lonergan's analysis of the breadth of theological method and its manifold operations, Pannenberg's theology promises to be a total program. It is a project of thought proposing an intellectual frame of reference of universal character. Neither of the two prefixes "re" or "de" is nearly adequate to the intention of Pannenberg's thought. "Re" suggests the past as containing the essential truth of things; "de" clears away the past to reveal the present as the moment of truth. Pannenberg holds to the priority of the future in our human encounter with reality;

This chapter is a slightly revised version of "Theology and Our Common World," published in *Worldview* (September, 1972), 22-27.

therefore, he would be more fond of words that begin with "pro" to suggest that the meaning of anything is determined by its relation to the whole of reality—the final future of all events. Words such as "promise" and "prolepsis" refer to the essential future which forms the universal horizon of meaning for all things in their concrete particularity.

Pannenberg is on his way to constructing a Christian world-view in modern terms. He is concerned both about the Christian legitimacy of the modern worldview and about the legitimacy of Christianity in the modern world. It is the right time, therefore, to ask the question whether a Christian *Weltanschauung* is possible. The dominant trends in modern theology— biblical, neo-orthodox, kerygmatic—have denied an essential relation between the Christian gospel and any worldview whatsoever. A Christian *Weltanschauung*—as also a Christian philosophy—is presumably impossible because the gospel is a word that frees a person from every worldview. It is as though a worldview has to be like a prison of myth and metaphysics, or of law and tradition, from which the gospel exists to free a person. The worldview provides a person with securities; the gospel drives a person into the world without securities. In this way modern Protestant theology of the kerygma rid itself of all questions dealing with worldview. The price it paid for this was to write off the whole world of nature and history as profane, i.e., theologically irrelevant. In the words of Rudolf Bultmann, "let those who have the modern worldview live as though they had none." Faith in the gospel is totally indifferent to all worldviews and to all such concerns.

Such a dichotomy between faith in the gospel and our view of the world has to be overcome. This is a chief concern of this volume. It has to be overcome for the sake of the gospel itself— its truth and integrity. Why? Because the gospel deals with the God of the Bible who is presented as the power to determine *all* reality. The idea of God cannot be separated from the whole of reality and truth without inflicting a mortal wound on its meaning. In this way the universality of theology comes into view. All non-theological materials are relevant to theological reflection, for there is no reality that can finally be understood on its own terms, if the reality of God as the Creator of the world and as the final Future of all things means anything at all. This is an ambitious undertaking, seemingly over-pretentious in an age that has assigned to theology a place not far removed from astrology, so far as the question of what can be seriously known is concerned. This is the question of the cognitive meaning and validity of theological statements. Pannenberg believes that a solid case can be made for theological knowledge in the open field of inquiry, discussion and argumentation.

The voice of Pannenberg was first heard within the highly parochial setting of a theological scrimmage on the doctrine of revelation. His initial thesis was inauspiciously propounded in an article, "Redemptive Event and History," in a neo-Lutheran journal of theology, *Kerygma und Dogma* (1959). Shortly thereafter Pannenberg edited a volume of essays, *Revelation as History,* supporting his thesis from the angle of other disciplines. He was on his way, partly because of the sharply onesided formulation of his historical conception of revelation, partly also because he laid bare vulnerable areas in the leading positions to the right (Karl Barth) and to the left (Rudolf Bultmann). Critics pounced on the seemingly excessive claims of the new theology: revelation is history happening, not some meaning hovering above and beyond the sphere of historical events; historical research as it is critically done today is capable of grasping the factual data which theology interprets in new situations; the resurrection of Jesus, surprising as it sounds, is such an historical event which can be established by the methods of critical investigation. The hostility and puzzlement that Pannenberg first aroused in theological circles have gradually yielded to better understanding and new expectations concerning his theological program. One hears of a growing number of Ph.D. students at many universities, here and abroad, focusing on Pannenberg's works, relating them to his intellectual heritage and our cultural milieu today. Perhaps these studies are premature. For although Pannenberg has written a large quantity of books and articles, he is surely just approaching mid-career. One knows from the study of other creative minds that many shifts and new interests develop even after the age of fifty!

The basic elements of Pannenberg's thought constitute the outline of a historicist metaphysics. Some theologians write monographs on special themes, without a total perspective that unifies them. That is the approach of the fragmentist. Others project a whole frame of reference within which all the fragments of knowledge are given a meaningful place in relation to

each other. This is the approach of Pannenberg. He is constructing a *Weltanschauung* friendly to the interests of history and
truth. In doing this he is drawing on the inherent universalism
of theology's own theme—the idea of God. Theology must be
universal in scope; all other intellectual enterprises that describe parts of the whole of reality must be taken up into the
universal perspective of theology.

At the same time Pannenberg is carrying on a criticism of
modern theological trends that focus on faith or the gospel
without relating them to a *Weltanschauung*. Truth is *one* in
the end, and that final unity of truth is to be found in God.
Therefore, a dualism in which theology sits in a corner thinking
about God, oblivious to the parade of the so-called secular disciplines passing by, must be overcome by a unifying vision that
does justice both to the partial truths of these disciplines and
the universal horizon of theology. To establish the legitimacy of
his outlook in dialog with the secular experience of reality and
conditions of inquiry today, Pannenberg follows a basic line of
hermeneutical thinking that runs from Schleiermacher through
Dilthey and Husserl and up to Heidegger and Gadamer. In this
stream of critical analysis of human understanding we find the
emergence of the most sophisticated secular mind. The challenge Pannenberg accepts is to demonstrate the meaningfulness
of theology in relation to the main premises of this secular
philosophy.

The question of meaning is where Pannenberg starts. It is a
starting point in agreement with the method of phenomenologi-
cal hermeneutics. This should not be seen in narrow theoretical
terms. For the broader cultural context has given birth to existentialist pessimism and its outcries of meaninglessness, anxiety, and
absurdity. Not only the heroes of Sartre's novels, but the youth
in our society feel themselves in a meaningless drift and as
members of groups going nowhere. Directionlessness and goal-
lessness are feelings that rob persons and societies of the sense of
meaning so essential to fulfilling life. The question of meaning
gives rise to the concern for context. Each of us experiences life
in bits and pieces—as fragments in a nexus of fragments. The
meaning of each fragment cannot be grasped as a thing in itself,
but only together with its wider context. Dilthey formulated
the key principle that "the single moment derives its meaning
from its connection with the whole." [1] This is decisive for the

theory of meaning. We cannot think and live without the category of meaning. But a reflection on meaning soon discloses that meaning is not an attribute of parts as such, but involves the *relation* of parts to the whole. Only knowledge of the whole can assign to the parts the meaning they possess. Gadamer's work demonstrates that the parts in question are historical in nature. Pannenberg concludes from this that the meaning of the historical parts derives from the whole of history. It is thus from an analysis of the conditions of meaning that Pannenberg reaches the notion of universal history. He also speaks of "the totality of history" or "history as a whole."

History, however, is an unfinished project. Humanity is still on its way. No one can yet possess the universal historical perspective, as though he were really standing at the end of history enjoying a retrospective grasp of all events and their essential meaning. Reality is not yet complete. All that is now is not the whole of what will be in the end. It is at this point that our much over-worked word "eschatology" comes into focus. Pannenberg is aware that the average Christian—and his secular brother —conjure up images of "life after death" and the "immortality of the soul" when the subject of eschatology arises. In the context of Pannenberg's theology eschatology means the end of history, not in the sense of a stop to it, but as its final goal. This idea was also suggested by Dilthey, though he never carried it through in his hermeneutical theory. Dilthey stated: "One would have to wait for the end of history to have all the material necessary to determine its meaning." Does this mean that man cannot know the meaning of anything at the present time, that all meaning must be postponed until the final future? Neither skepticism nor pessimism pervades Pannenberg's system of thought. The mind has the capacity of running ahead of the present through anticipation. As in Heidegger's thought a person can run ahead *(vorzulaufen)* to the *eschaton* of his life and live the present in that light, so for Pannenberg the final whole of all reality can already now be present and meaningful through anticipation.

The future aspect of eschatology was forcefully brought to the fore in the gospel research of Albert Schweitzer. Pannenberg latches on to that, since he regards it as theologically significant. But, as we have seen, the future aspect also arises as the horizon of meaning in the process of history. From the word itself, of course, it would seem that the idea of a *future* eschatology is a pleonasm—a redundant expression. We grasp the eschatological future only in a partial and provisional way. The whole truth can never be fully expressed within the finite structures of human knowing, yet it is that truth that is present in our partial understanding and fragmentary thoughts. In the future these present apprehensions of truth will prove to be inadequate and new cognitive perspectives will arise. In this way the categories of immanence and transcendence are applied to a historico-eschatological system of reality and scheme of knowledge.

When the early Christian gospel made its way into the world of Greek metaphysical philosophy, it achieved a synthesis that framed a worldview shaped by the doctrine of God. Modern Protestant theology, in the famous words of Harnack, has called this the Hellenization of Christianity. The school of Albrecht Ritschl, followed by Karl Barth and Emil Brunner, demanded a thorough-going elimination of the metaphysical elements in the patristic synthesis (the theology of the church fathers of the first five centuries). This synthesis was continued by the Middle Ages, also by the Reformation and post-Reformation theologies, until it was attacked and demolished, first by critical philosophy (Kant) and then by biblical theology (Barth and Cullmann). Pannenberg agrees with the judgment that the traditional doctrine of God linked itself to Greek metaphysics. But this was not in principle a mistake. In fact, the universal claim of the God of Israel, being the one true God, compelled Christian theology to make its witness *also* in philosophical terms. However, whether this was done altogether successfully is another question. Pannenberg thinks not. The biblical witness to the freedom of God, freely acting in the course of historical events, did not achieve appropriate expression in the philosophical categories of that time. But the task itself was and is legitimate, as an expression of the universal claim of the Judaeo-Christian God. The task is to penetrate and transform critically the philosophical concept of God in light of the biblical God of freedom and futurity, the God of hope and history. But this biblical perspective does not call for less universality than the patristic theologians attempted, but rather for a reworking of the philosophical doctrine of God without abandoning the heritage of a critically interpreted metaphysics.

The collapse of the traditional Christian *Weltanschauung,*

with the idea of God as the main subject of history and nature, of church and society, is a fact that cannot be denied. Whether this is a matter over which to rejoice or to regret can be left to a person's subjectivity. But it is a fact with world-historical consequences; it is also a fact that no functional equivalent has arisen to take its place. There is no total framework of meaning which assigns to things their place in the plot, no vision of holiscopic destiny that directs the dynamisms that drive history— no "predestination." The laughing of the secular mentality at the loss of the overarching canopy of meaning that the Christian worldview once provided is not to be taken at face value. A case of gallows humor? Whistling in the dark?

Pannenberg is in no way calling for a romantic retrieval of the Christian worldview that commanded even the basic loyalties and shaped the futurist vision of the great thinkers of the Enlightenment. It is more a question of going forward to a new construction, which is not a reconstruction but a pre-construction of the shape of coming things, in their essential future. In this way theology can do for our time what the thinkers of the Enlightenment and of German idealism tried as a matter of principle to do for their time, namely, to construct a total synthesis of meaning in which biblical truth is somehow put together with the most enlightened reason of modern times. It must be reason with ecstasy and transcendency inherent in its flight, not a reason that flies close to the ground with clipped wings.

Will it be a desirable thing for reason once again to project a worldview—imaginative yet reasonable, provisional yet meaningful—within the total horizon of which the scattered fragments, the odd parts, bits and pieces of experience, can be sustained in basic trust that they possess significance in the ultimate scheme of things? I think it is a risky thing for theology to attempt. Might it not run amuck the warning about gaining the whole world and losing one's soul? Was this not the crux of Kierkegaard's crusade against Hegel and of Barth's against 19th century Protestant theology? No doubt it was. But I think the risk is worth taking, not only because one might feel that with Pannenberg the project is in good hands, but because there is a dreadfully serious ministry that needs to be carried out in a sick and perhaps dying culture. Theology could have therapeutic meaning in a culture that suffers from future-neurosis, future-shock, or whatever one may call the present mood. If theology will not carry out this mission today, then the culture at large will lay its eggs in the nests of other birds. In the wake of the collapsing Christian worldview, other movements with hybristic claims to universality gathered up all the scattered fragments into their total systems of interpretation, only these did not have the self-critical and self-relativizing impulses coming from their very foundations. In contrast Christianity has repeatedly raised up its own critics from within, fighting against every tendency to absolutize itself. Movements such as fascism, communism, and scientific humanism have offered themselves as the new gods, after the old ones have fled. These are worldviews that generate idolatry in their very essence. For this very reason there is no way for the biblical message to stay out of the competition among the worldviews at work in history. The trick is for a worldview to be a servant of meaning and freedom for man in history, rather than a master in control of his thoughts and actions. The ontological basis of such a worldview is Pannenberg's idea of God as the power of the future that moves in history as the source of freedom and newness. It drives man to transcend every state of affairs, to be open to the future of God whose essence is pure freedom. This is the *principium*—the ontological principle—which is at once at the heart of the Christian message and the starting point of a possible Christian *Weltanschauung*.

Theology should find it no longer amusing that its gospel has exercised a purely negative iconoclastic effect on the worldviews of modern man. Where men have not been swept into other total networks of meaning in history, they have been abandoned to a miserable emptiness—without either the gospel or other gods. There is as it were a vacuum of meaningful images and goals, no map, no signs, no journey, no perspective, no orientation, only a repulsive amount of nothing. Neither a person nor a culture can exist meaningfully without a frame of reference, without a vision of the whole that bestows confidence that man is not alone in a world of facts without values, motions without meanings, demons without angels, process without purpose, play without joy, futurity without fulfillment, etc. This breakdown of the comprehensive unity of all things in their ultimate and essential future is what happens when man becomes the only subject and subject matter of history. The doctrine of the his-

toricity of man in existentialist philosophy was intended to liberate man from all worldviews and total systems. The result,
however, was the interpretation of history without God, therefore also without a meaningful goal, without an expectation of
a fulfilling future of life. Pannenberg doubts, in fact, he denies
that history can be meaningfully interpreted in its uniqueness
and continuity without the notion that God is the bearer of
history; history is the history of God in the largest sense of its
meaning. Otherwise it breaks up into segments and fragments.
"It is the horizon of world history which first makes it possible
to appreciate the full significance of an individual event." [2]
Without world history there is no meaning in history. The connection between contingent events in history is grounded in the
transcendent unity of God, as their common universal future.
In this way the idea of God is indispensable for the historian
who does not restrict himself to detailed research of small segments of happenings.

Pannenberg is fighting on two wide fronts in modern culture—
existentialism and positivism. These moods and movements have
made deep inroads into theology, forcing it to retreat behind
the lines, and to hide away in sheltered havens, forsaking its
own world-historical horizon. Breaking the worldview in Western culture brought dark clouds of doom and depression into
the present and a fatal break with the past. The realm of the
future carried the stench of death in iconoclastic existentialism.
No hopeful images of the future were retained—no immortality,
resurrection, world renewal, or fulfilling endstate. There is only
existence in the present, condemned to the Sisyphean fate of
rolling a heavy burden uphill with no hope of reaching the top,
and with nothing there to greet him. Not only the glory of God
has faded away into nothingness, but the glory of man has become jaded by endless boredom. Days and nights roll on in a
dreary desert state of a nihilized future enclosing man in a uni-
dimensional timeless present. At this point Pannenberg's insis-
tence on the eschatological future as the horizon of existential,
social, and world-historical meaning is calculated to meet head-
on the existentialist themes of meaninglessness and futureless-
ness. Nihilism, pessimism, and fatalism have never released any
power to create something new and interesting under the sun.
They spell individual and cultural suicide. Therefore the question of worldview is a survival issue, a matter of life and death.

The biblical message of life cannot keep warm by its own fire, watching the surrounding culture pound nails into its own coffin. Biblical faith cannot be imprisoned in any existing *Weltanschauung,* but in a pioneering way it throws open new dimensions, sponsoring change, always keeping its own viewpoints moving in history. The elements of the worldview that Pannenberg is constructing are not parts of a closed, fixed, and rigidly self-sufficient system. His image of the eschatological future of universal history breaks through the frontiers of time that threaten to close down history, putting men at the mercy of the tyranny of an absolute system or the tyranny of time contracting into a totally empty almighty NOW. This image of the future brings value into the present while keeping it relative, provisional and open to new things.

On the other front is the all-pervasive spirit of positivism in which the future of novelty expires in a flattened out world without myth and metaphysics, without divinity and transcendence. If the eschatological and metaphysical dimensions of human consciousness have been put out of commission, will the spirit of man be able to thrive in the petrified soil that remains? Can there be any nourishment for the roots of human aesthetic sensibilities and spiritual sensitivities in the rock-hard positivism that has spread into philosophy and science, and into society and the university? Pannenberg is taking his theology into these areas, willing to argue its merits in face of the credentialing process to which they at least pay lip service. That is why reason and not faith is the place where theology gets on the pike where all the traffic in human affairs runs together. Faith is voided of special noetic significance—as a category of special revelational knowledge—in order to emphasize its character as trust in God, as a way of orienting life to the future in trust and openness.

It is a serious question whether theology can break the neck of a positivism which rules out in advance the elements of freedom, novelty, uniqueness, contingency, unity, universality, transcendency, all of which are entailed in Christian language about the one God freely acting as the power to determine the essential meaning and future of all things in nature and history! The influence of the natural sciences swelled to the extent that the cultural sciences gave way to the use of quantification and mathematics and to value-free judgments on the part of the researchers. Science became swollen and conscience began to shrink. By throwing over a worldview that can unite both science and conscience in a higher unity, a crisis sets into science itself. The question is now being dealt with in full earnest as to what science is, what it ought to be, its task and responsibility, its place and function in culture. Scientific humanism expected to deliver the salvation on earth that the world religions deferred to another world. The progress in the battle against disease and hunger and in mastering control over the elements of nature seemed to increase incredibly. But how much closer has it brought mankind to the utopia of tomorrow—life without hate and poverty, without war and hunger, without injustice and inequality? The crisis in science is due in part to the growing awareness, also on the part of scientists, that the science in a culture benefits first and foremost those in control. Science is class-power in the hands of the highest bidders. Pure science, like pure religion, is an abstraction. Actually, there are scientists who will take on any job, if there is money behind it. Like others they work hard for bread. "He who pays the piper calls the tune." In our day, that is government, industry, advertising, entertainment, perhaps also big crime laboratories, as certain radicals have called the universities. In relation to this concept of "hired science" it is so essential to develop in our society elements of a common worldview in which the moral decisions that condition the social future of mankind can be taken by responsible agents who understand each other.

Nowhere should there be a greater opportunity for responsible thinkers to develop a common horizon of meaning for all the specialized compartments of knowledge than the university. In Pannenberg's theology universality is its special theme; the idea of a *uni*versity presupposes theology as the essential condition of its possibility. "Theology is a universal science," says Pannenberg. He charges much of modern theology with having neglected its universal task, willing instead to confine itself to being one positive science among a plethora of specialized disciplines. This led to an estrangement between theology and the secular sciences, theology getting the worst of it. Pannenberg is calling for theology to advance, as it first did in the patristic era, into the universal consciousness of truth, as a way of giving expression to what it means by the word "God."

Does the university need theology? Does it need a discipline

performing the intellectual task of speaking of God in relation
to the totality of reality, the special parts of which are investi-
gated by the non-theological disciplines in a university? This
sounds almost preposterous, when one considers a modern American university of over 40,000 students in which the discipline
of theology is totally absent from the curriculum. This is almost
the rule, not the exception. Pannenberg is convinced that this
condition does not bespeak the health of the university. He is
not among those who—like Ivan Illich—claim to hear the hoof-
beats of the apocalyptic riders approaching the gates of the modern university. After all, in his country theology continues to
enjoy a place of dignity in the university, though perhaps not
as queen of the sciences. But what about the tremendously huge
universities in America? The catalogues promise that almost anything can be bought over the university counters, out of an
impressive inventory of science and technology. But what do all
the scraps add up to? Does the university provide a framework
of meaning—a *Weltanschauung*—for all the sub-specialties that
turn out scattered fragments of knowledge? Are not students
complaining that they are becoming, as it were, scatter-brains
who gather up a lot of parts without comprehending the whole
to which they are connected? Is it not a lack of the sense of the
whole that makes the scraps of learning seem so strikingly
pointless? Goethe's *Faust* was prophetic: "Dann hat er die
Teile in seiner Hand. Fehlt leider! nur das geistiger Band."
It was a prophecy that has come true a century and a half later.
What good does it do if we can split the atom and lose the
universe of meaning? If we can master microphysics and get lost
in the macrocosm?

The present-day strategy is to overcome the overblown specialties by interdisciplinary alliances. It won't work. A collection of academic splinters cannot be glued together to make an
integrated whole worthy of the name of university. It is a matter
of worldview—a question of *Weltanschauung*. An unkind re-
viewer once dismissed one of Pannenberg's books under the title,
"Turning Back the Clock!" The idea of a theological worldview, involving a full scale metaphysics, epistemology, and
philosophy of history, will strike many readers as a romantic
dream about the good old days when theology ruled from on
high. But that is not our contention. The role of theology is
much more humble. It would enter not as tyrant with privileged

authority, but as a servant-healer working out continuities of meaning, referring parts to a whole frame of reference, and integrating the threads of human learning into a total tapestry of knowledge. The results will not be final, certainly always fluid and in motion, provisional and relative, yet promising and meaningful enough.

One cannot read far in Pannenberg's writings without being impressed by the strength of his own drive to know the whole truth and to view things from the most comprehensive viewpoint that is presently attainable. He issues frequent and strong warnings to his fellow theologians not to imagine that the quest for truth is an easy trip that one can make by an arbitrary "leap of faith." He will not allow theology to withdraw into a ghetto to carry on a separate conversation, as though it could long survive in the modern world by coiling itself protectively around a special revelation it keeps to itself. His call to enter the open forum of intellectual discussion is not, however, taking the form of the reductionistic de-process, of making the gospel relevant to modern times at all costs. It is a new synthesis, with too much of the old thesis for the modernists, and too much of the current antithesis for the conservatives. But Pannenberg is at home with neither one nor the other. On the American scene he is perhaps the most read and talked about theologian, not among the laity, to be sure, but among the theologians who are themselves working out their own new syntheses.

4

Death and
the Resurrection
of Jesus

Introduction — Death in Our Time

Somewhere I saw this graffito: "So many people now die who never died before." This is a reminder that death has become a focal point of interest in the early seventies. We can imagine two plausible reasons for this. First of all, death is in any case a lonely event; it is lonelier still in a mass technological society. The feeling that "nobody knows my name" is widespread in our time. Secondly, we are members of an affluent nation that mass produces and exports ghastly instruments designed to kill. The feeling that we are directly guilty of the death of millions of innocent people around the world weighs heavily on our conscience. We are rapidly becoming a death-oriented people. Killing is big business; or—big business is killing. As Americans we are into it very deeply.

This is the second time in our century when the horizon of death has enfolded us like a sky of black clouds. The First World War provided the background against which Martin Heidegger, Jean-Paul Sartre, and their fellow existentialists interpreted human existence as "being-toward-death" and nothingness. They called for sheer courage in face of the anxiety of death. People were no longer ashamed to admit their fears. They talked about death and anxiety with a new honesty. Now again, after a decade and more of a terrible war, the face of death is calling for a new seriousness, awakening conscience and arousing care.

Early in the First World War Sigmund Freud published two essays entitled, *Timely Thoughts on War and Death*, in 1915. Note what he wrote at that time: "The war has disturbed our previous relation to death. This relation was not sincere. If one listened to us, we were, of course, ready to declare that death is the necessary end of all life, that every one of us owed nature his own death and must be prepared to pay this debt—in short, that death is natural, undeniable, and unavoidable. In reality, however, we used to behave as if it were different. We have shown the unmistakable tendency to push death aside, to eliminate it from life. We have tried to keep a deadly silence about death." [1]

The silence about death has been broken. War has the effect of revealing death as the eschaton of life. A person becomes aware in his guts that death is the end. Or better, he becomes aware that he must die his own death, and that nobody can do it for him. The many cloaks that our culture places over death are ripped off when the shock of war personalizes death as one's very own death. When that happens, we want to talk about it honestly. This could very well be the major purpose of a theology of death and resurrection—to help us to face death and to talk about it without self-deception.

A Phenomenology of Death

Nobody knows about death from his own personal experience. Each person knows that he will die—and die just once—by observing the law of mortality at work all around him. Death is not something that he can experience and survive to tell about.

How can we talk about death, then, as a phenomenon if it lies beyond the range of our experience? How can there be a phenomenology of death? The answer is that we do have a sort of experience of death, that is, through the power of anticipatory imagination. We anticipate death as the absolutely certain end to life. That is all we really know about it. It is the counter-pole to life. A person is dead or alive. There is no in-between third state.

Death is the great equalizer. We all know equally much about it. There are no professors who can specialize in death and teach courses *on* it. They can only deal with data that surround it. Every person is his own expert when it comes to his own dying. There is no one around we can consult to instruct us on what it is like. Dying, on the other hand, is something we can research. We can listen to what the dying say about the death they anticipate, as Dr. Elizabeth Kübler-Ross has so expertly done in her book, *Death and Dying*. But there is an infinite gulf between death and dying. We can all do lots of dying, but that does not make us dead yet. Dying is a process that is continually going on within us. Death is a final fate. We anticipate death as a definitive catastrophic event that attacks us from the outside. This is underscored by the French phenomenologist, Paul Ricoeur, who says: "Death is not in me like life—and like suffering, aging, and contingence—it always remains a stranger." [2] We sense that we do not find death in ourselves, but rather that it is an inimical power with roots lying outside ourselves. This is an intuitive feeling expressed in such classical symbols as the "angel of death" in the Old Testament and as a "rider on a pale horse" in the New Testament. In the history of literature and art, death is variously depicted as a scythe or sword or inverted torch.

Yet, this death which is most strange to us, most antithetical to our very being, is at the same time our most intimate and inwardly certain destiny. Death is indeed a stranger, as Ricoeur says. But its strangeness is something to which we are fatefully bound. Augustine said: *"Incerta omnia, sola mors certa."* Everything is uncertain, with the sole exception of death. We do not know when, but it is absolutely inescapable. *Hora incerta, mors certa.* This stranger to our being is our own most certain future. As we say so often, "It is sure to be the death of me." We mean that it will put an end to us. It will wipe us out. Death is a deadly occurrence.

Transcending Death

It is precisely because we pre-view death as the final and definitive end of life that we begin to question whether there is any way to transcend it. We know that death is the end, but religion is born to negate and transcend it. This is religion as hope expressing itself in such traditional symbols as immortality of the soul or resurrection of the dead. Sigmund Freud, in the essay we have already quoted, wrote that, "At bottom, nobody believes in his own death. Or, and this is the same: In his unconsciousness, every one of us is convinced of his immortality." [3]

Now what about the image of immortality? This is not a specifically Christian answer to the question of hope for a death-transcending future. It can be found in many religions, but it made its entrance into the Christian tradition by way of Platonic anthropology. We could say that Plato unforgettably enveloped the death of his beloved Socrates with the hope of immortality. In Plato's *Apology* he has Socrates facing death with the prospect of gaining a future state better than this life. One can almost feel the excitement of hope-filled conviction in the words: "To die is gain." Or this: "If death is the journey to another place, and there, as men say, all the dead abide, what good, O my friends and judges, can be greater than this?" [4]

It seems as though the history of religion can be interpreted as the story of hope to transcend death as the ultimate limit of human finitude. Man knows that he is bound to die and that death confronts him as an obstacle threatening to frustrate his hope for fulfillment. If death is the final verdict that befalls human striving, then hope for a totally human, communal, and cosmic fulfillment is all in vain. Then the future spells a miscarriage of hope. If hope in its fullest scope is awaiting a future of personal fulfillment, and if the only future that one can conjure up is death, then hope is totally negated. Then hope is smitten in its very heart. The resultant mood inevitably becomes one of hopelessness; it gives rise to a feeling of meaninglessness. Perhaps one will be inclined to make the most of it, and shout: "Eat, drink, and be merry, for tomorrow we die." But, as the poet has said, "hope springs eternal in the human breast." This means that the thrust of hope attacks the threat of death. Man is structured heuristically as hope—hope in quest of fulfillment. It belongs to man's nature to hope for fulfillment beyond death. That is the truth about man that Plato was conveying by his doctrine of the immortality of the soul. He postulated a future for the soul of man that transcended death. He did not use the symbol of the resurrection, as in Christian eschatology, but the idea of immortality to express man's hope for participation in the power of life that conquers even death.

The Greek Fathers in the ancient church appropriated the Platonic notion of immortality, but invested it with certain specifically Christian ideas. They did not deny that man must face death. Man comes from dust and returns to dust. They taught that there was nothing *naturally* immortal about man. They, in fact, reiterated the biblical teaching that "the wages of sin is death." At the same time these early Fathers affirmed that man may share in the power of life that overcomes death. To share in this divine life, man must eat the divine food. He must receive the medicine of immortality, the *pharmakon athanasias.* Thus,

what we call "holy communion" was a sacred meal that com-
municates immortality, for there believers could eat the immortal body of their divine Lord and drink his blood. This is the
power of immortality to overcome the death-ridden finitude
of man.

In modern theology the Platonic idea of the immortality of
the soul has been severely criticized. Also the Patristic synthesis,
which fused the biblical symbol of resurrection of the body with
the Greek idea of immortality of the soul, has been subject to
searching criticism. It is not uncommon for Protestant theology
since Adolf von Harnack to call for a thorough de-Platonization
of the theology produced by the Fathers during the first five
centuries of Christianity. The motive is chiefly for the sake of
a fuller recovery of the New Testament belief in resurrection.
The assumption is that resurrection hope and belief in immortality stand in sharp contrast to each other. We would agree
with this judgment, with the proviso that both are rooted in a
common structure of existence. Both are images of hope, rooted
in man's very nature to press on beyond every fixed limit con-
fronting him, in spite of the inescapability of the fate of death.
But today the idea of the immortality of the soul, however self-
evident to Plato and the main stream of the Western philosophical tradition, no longer expresses the self-understanding of modern man. Its chief difficulty is the separation of body and soul
that it entails. There is no existence of a soul apart from the
body; they form a unity of being and action. They are the
outer and the inner aspects of the *whole* person. Theologically,
however, the more telling argument is that the Platonic idea of
immortality does not take death seriously. In Socrates' speech to
the Athenians, he speaks of death as a liberation of the soul, not
as a negation. Death is positively evaluated, bearing a friendly
face ready to greet man at the end of his life. Not so with Jesus.
He enters into death in great pain, uttering a loud cry, "It is
finished."

Death and Mortality

In modern times many people face death without the ministry
of hope. The acids of secularism have eroded the symbols of
hope, whether the Greek idea of immortality or the Christian
belief in resurrection. Nor is it the case that modern man, with-

out hope for eternal life, is visibly doubled over with cramps for
fear of death. There is, of course, no uniform model of the
modern man. Many people live a superficial life and refuse to
raise the question about death. Others suppress the question, or
drown it out with drugs, noise, sex, busy-ness, or anything else
that works to numb the nerves that keep man sensitive to his
own deathly fate. This is perhaps the common way of the un-
reflective secular person in our day. But, on the other hand,
many thinking people simply see no need for any images of
hope for lasting life beyond death. They are not seized by great
anxiety about having to die; their days do not become boring
and full of ennui as their approaching end draws nearer. They
look upon death as a perfectly natural thing. Walter Kaufmann,
for example, writes as though there is nothing to fear in death.
He accuses Christianity of having exercised "its vast influence
to make men dread death." [5] This attitude would change, he
avers, if we would be given the assurance that when we die, our
world simply ends and there is absolutely nothing we shall miss.
Kaufmann says, "He that has made something of his life can
face death without anxiety." [6] This is said in criticism of existentialism; for in existentialism death triggers moods of dread,
despair and anxiety.

Kaufmann is representing what we may call the naturalistic
view of death. The death of man is not the "wages of sin" but
merely the necessary end of every creature within the eco-system
of nature. Everything that is born and lives must also die and
be recycled into the earth, later perhaps to become food for other
creatures. While we live, we eat cattle and pigs and fish and
shrimps; when we die, we are eaten by germs and worms. What
we call "life" seems to be so arranged that it eats itself to death.
Human life is no exception to this natural process.

It is impossible to deny the element of truth in this naturalistic interpretation of death. Therefore, we should perhaps
introduce a distinction between mortality and death. In terms of
the grounding of man's life in this vital material universe, it is
perfectly natural and inevitable that man will share in the physio-
logical process of decay and disintegration.

When the mortality of man is viewed in the light of nature,
the phenomenon of death poses neither terror nor mystery. For
within the vegetative and animal spheres, life and death are mu-

tually implicative; each presupposes the other. But man does not live by this viewpoint alone. It seems too superficial to the person who contemplates the pain and distress implied in his own dying. No amount of assurance that death is natural can dispell the despair that accompanies it. If death is purely natural, and nothing more, then why do people flee from their death? Or why do they work so hard to drum up a heroic attitude? The reason is that death is more than mortality. Death is ambiguous. It is a form of necessity; we must die; we are essentially mortal.

Death is a mark of our finitude as creatures who exist together with the whole creation. My mortality is a basic component of my finitude in this em-bodied human condition. What is not given as a component of my finitude, but is rather a mark of my sinfulness, my fallen human condition, is the fact that this mortality achieves a kind of deadly hypostatic power over against my freedom to be a human being. Hence its terrifying and destructive character! I am afraid to die. I become afraid of my mortality, because I am not free; I am in bondage to death; it holds me captive. Mere natural mortality has become death (*thanatos* in the sense of St. Paul). It is this mortality *qua* death that the Bible calls the "wages of sin." This biblical phrase is therefore not contrary to the naturalistic view of death, which is the governing hypothesis of the modern life sciences. Instead, the idea of death as the wages of sin points to the two-dimensional phenomenon of death; it points to the deadliness of death in human existence.

Mortality as such is not sinful or evil; it is merely the mark of human finitude. But mortality becomes powerfully deadly and aligned with sin when it becomes the orientation point of one's life. Mortality becomes death when one lives by its criteria, when one seeks to gain his life from it, or spends his lifetime denying or disguising it. In this way one can be in bondage to death as a power that holds the swaying influence in one's living. Then it is the final enemy of man that must be destroyed. The good news of the resurrection in the New Testament is linked to this deadly quality of man's mortality. The resurrection, as we shall see, is no exemption from mortality. Rather, it presupposes it. It is not an event to deny mortality, but to rob mortality of its biting and binding effect in the lives of men.

Resurrection Hope

Christian hope is based on the gospel of the resurrection of Jesus of Nazareth, because in this event God released the power of his own living future beyond the finality of death. If Jesus would not have been raised from the dead, his own earthly ministry would not have been raised to the highest power in the history of salvation. His fate would have been merely that of another heroic prophet. The crucifixion of Jesus could not of itself have nourished great hope for the future of the cause that he proclaimed and lived. This cause was the coming of the kingdom of God and the rule of his righteousness throughout the whole of creation. Jesus' claim to be the prime representative of this cause on earth would have been nullified had he been utterly defeated by death. But God vindicated and ratified his claim to be the authoritative mediator of his kingdom by raising him from the dead, thus promising that the cause of Jesus would still enjoy a future in world history. The church of Jesus the Christ is the instrument by which God is futurizing the cause of Jesus in world history. That is its essential role and function. Jesus the Christ could hardly have been announced as the chief cornerstone of the church apart from his entry into a new and deathless form of life through the resurrection. He is called the Christ, the promised Messiah, because he assumed the role of breaking through the barrier of this old and dying age into the new reality of God's rule.

Resurrection hope points us ahead to what we cannot see and have never experienced. We do not really know what reality is to which the symbol of the resurrection refers. It is more than the revivification of the physical body of the crucified Jesus. If it were just that, Jesus would not be unlike a Lazarus, who was reported to have returned to life three days after his death. But Lazarus had to die again; his return to life did not transcend the conditions of this mortal life. The resurrection of Jesus, in contrast, was an eschatological occurrence, an event above and beyond the enclosure of death. It is the beginning of something really new; it means a living union of the crucified Jesus with God himself, so that he can continue to be the representative of God to man and of man to God now and forever.

Because God has raised Jesus from the dead, we have good reason to hope for lasting life, in spite of the "axe of annihilation" (Bloch) that swings above all of us. It is the good news of "in spite of." *In spite of* the jaws of death that swallow us up in the end, *in spite of* the negativities of existence that defeat us now, *in spite of* the unfulfilled state of every living thing, there is reason to hope for Christ's sake. We know we have to die, yet on account of Christ we hope and trust that the word of life is more powerful in the end than death. We hope for a lasting future of our personal identity, as well as life together with all those whom love embraces.

It is this word of resurrection hope that prevails against the doubt and nihilism that tempt us to despair and self-destruction. It may be that for some modern secular people, death is nothing more than a biological incident. But personally I doubt that modern man distinguishes himself any better than primitive or medieval man in face of death. I think he's really scared to death of death. Else why do we moderns pay the mortician an absurd amount of money to camouflage it and make a dead person look life-like? Why do we give a person an expensive ride to the cemetery in a big black limousine after he's dead? Why do we use so many euphemisms to refer to death, like "passing on" and "going home"? Modern man does not live victoriously in face of death with a resurrection hope. And he has put nothing in its place that can put the deathly power of death to death. He has nothing that can match the resurrection hope in countering the deadliness of death with the promise of life eternal.

The power of resurrection hope rests upon two conditions— that it happened to Jesus and that it means what the New Testament kerygma says. Beyond this there is lots of room for interpretation and speculation. We do not know *what* really happened; we are committed to the belief *that* it happened. We do know that it means that in raising Jesus from the dead, God promises to give life to the dead and to call into existence the things that do not exist. We do not have a theory to explain it; we do not know how it happened. There is an element of agnosticism in the Christian belief in resurrection. We are not ashamed to say we do not know all things, or even that we do not know some essential things. We are willing to wait in hope also for future insight and illumination. The knowledge of faith awaits also its doxological future and fulfillment, to the glory of God the Father who will in the end be all in all.

The Scope of Hope

The hope of the resurrection concerns the individual person. But its meaning is wider in scope. It embraces hope for the world, for the whole world, not merely for the individual. Yet, it is proper to emphasize that resurrection does relate to the question of personal identity and hope for fulfillment. In an age of collectivism, in which no less a thinker than B. F. Skinner prophecies a future "beyond freedom and dignity," it is important to stress that hope for personal fulfillment can never be translated into the good of the whole. The mere promise of a better society in the future does not proffer a real fulfillment of the individual, for the reason that the meaning of a person is not equatable with his contribution to the social process. His meaning as a person is not exhausted by all the roles that he plays in society. Resurrection hope, as the New Testament announces it, strives for a total personal fulfillment.

The important thing to stress, however, is that the assurance of personal identity-in-fulfillment makes a difference in the life of the person now. Eschatological hope is not merely something for the future.

Eschatology is the Christian doctrine of the future of God. It is not primarily a doctrine of the "last things" that will pile up at the end of history, millions or billions of years from now. That would void it of existential significance in the present. God is the power of the future becoming present now. The resurrection is the event which releases the future of life into this body of death. The future of fulfillment which was embodied in Jesus of Nazareth is communicated to those who believe in his name.

The personal meaning of participation through faith and hope in the risen Christ is the acquisition of a transcendent source of life beyond the questionable values of any existing religion, morality, or culture. It yields to a person the power of relativizing all concrete historical forms so that they remain open and flexible, and do not become traps or idols. The power of the resurrection in personal life conquers the feeling that a person's life is lived for nought; it gives a sense of a meaningful outcome of life, of worthwhileness to one's efforts in spite of their partial and ambiguous character. Society and all its glory cannot guarantee the absolute significance of each individual;

it usually favors the stronger people. The little ones are crushed beneath the steamrollers of history. But even the strongest ones are replaceable and exchangeable. When John F. Kennedy was president, he was the most powerful man on earth. When he died, there were eager and willing people to take his place. That is the lot that befalls every person under the conditions of existence, even the most powerful rulers in world history. The message of the resurrection speaks to this human predicament. It is a message of victory over death, suffering, and pointless striving. This message is a source of transcendence that this world cannot give. It mediates love, healing, freedom, and righteousness which man longs for now but cannot attain on his own. Nothing in this world can satisfy that hunger. In simplest terms, a person is endowed with an unlimited desire to be wholly human, but he experiences life as an unmitigated series of frustrated efforts that fall short of the goal.

On account of the resurrection of Jesus, the value of human life becomes boundless and infinite. It inflates the price of human life beyond every kind of currency exchange in this world. Man cannot be adequately defined in his being and meaning with sole reference to himself. The truth of the resurrection is that man is the creature who surpasses himself, not by his own reason and strength, but through the agency and mercy of the man Jesus and his Spirit, in whom and through whom God is really present. Man is not the measure of man; only God is. To be truly human is therefore not to be turned in and enclosed upon oneself; it is to be open to the absolute future and to participate in the pure freedom of God. In this direction we can achieve a more adequate definition of man. Man cannot be adequately defined with too low a ceiling placed on his potential. He is a creature in quest of a total unburdening, a full freedom, and liberation from every bondage.

So much for the personal meaning of resurrection hope. But its scope is wider. This is a *total hope;* it embraces the future of society and the world. There is a universalism of hope. At the end God will be all in all, totally present in everyone and everything, and they totally fulfilled with each other and in him. That is Paul's vision impregnated by hope. It is no small hope that clings to the mere salvation of the individual soul. It is more than existential and personal. Communal and cosmic dimensions are projected by the imagination of hope. The

Christian imbued with love does not hope merely for himself, his family and friends, and let the rest go to hell. Not only by *nature* but more especially by *grace,* if we can still make such a distinction at all, the Christian person knows himself to be in solidarity with the whole family of mankind and the whole creation. For this reason the artistic imagination is liberated to find expressions and paint pictures that go beyond individual personal fulfillment.

Resurrection hope points to eschatological fulfillment; it speaks the language of symbols. Spatial and temporal images are used to depict the fulfilling future anticipated by hope. Bodily and spiritual ills are healed. This healing has personal as well as social dimensions. Nobody can be healed by himself; a person experiences healing in a psycho-social field of reality. When one member suffers, the whole body of mankind is in pain. The sickness of one is a symptom of the unhealthy condition of the whole. Perspectives on the relation between an individual person and his social community are thus implied in the large vision of Christian hope.

Similarly, insights concerning the vital relations between men and the material world are released by this larger vision. Not only the history of mankind, but also the history of nature is heir to the promise of fulfillment in the Bible, especially in the apocalyptic portions of Scripture. The gospel is not good news for man and bad news for the cosmos. Man is in continuity with nature. Ultimately the forward movement of the material world and the history of personal and social life converge on the same ultimate goal. This goal is the Omega-Point, in the cosmic vision of Teilhard de Chardin's theology. I affirm this vision as an imaginative recapitulation of the wide scope of hope in the Bible; it incorporates the future of man and the cosmos within the horizon of their common destiny in the eternal plenitude of God.

5

Basic Polarities of the Gospel Message

In a little brochure by Peter Berger, entitled "Letter on the Parish Ministry," he is writing to a college senior who is considering entering a seminary to study for the parish ministry. The student is honestly wondering whether the ministry is not a very dismal affair. He is terribly worried about entering a ministry so "irrelevant" to the modern man, so "ineffective" in changing the world and "morally ambiguous" because of the compromises the institutional church makes with the evil power structures. To top it off, the ministry is "absurd," because its message hardly squares with reason, truth or common sense. Irrelevant, ineffective, morally ambiguous, and generally absurd —who cares to have anything to do with the ministry bag? Berger is obviously feeling a bit uneasy from the start, because this pre-seminarian may have gotten such ideas from reading Berger's own books, such as *The Noise of Solemn Assemblies, The Precarious Vision,* and *The Sacred Canopy.* If Berger can say so many nasty things about the church and its ministry in these books, how would he now counsel a person who is wondering whether to blow his future on just such a profession?

As it turns out, Peter Berger does a pretty good job of answering. He grants the student the truth of all the adjectives, but he points to something that hopefully makes it all worthwhile. That is the unique gospel of Jesus Christ—the story that God has turned toward the world of mankind in love and is now acting to save it. This is what evangelism is all about—the gospel of salvation. But what is the gospel? The question brings us to the first of the *basic polarities* of the gospel message—the subject of this chapter.

69

An Ultimate and Universal Message

The gospel of Jesus Christ is an *ultimate* message that concerns the very last thing that a human being can hope for; yet, at the same time, it is a *universal* message that embraces the meaning of all the next to the last—the penultimate—things that can concern a person. Negatively stated, the gospel cannot be understood in a monistic frame of reference, but only in terms of the polar opposition between this world and the coming world (Eph. 1:20). The gospel is not merely a thing of the present, nor a thing of the future; rather, it announces the future with the power to shape the present. It is not useful, therefore, to join the tug of war between those who refer the gospel wholly to matters of this present world or defer it to mansions in some other world. The content of the gospel is the power of God in Jesus Christ to mediate the newness of the coming kingdom into the frame of this present world, to change it from within and through the historical sequence of events. The gospel is the event that keeps this world and the coming kingdom from separating into two opposite worlds, one coming after the other, so that even now there is an overlapping of the old by the new, until finally the old shall fade away to reveal the glory of God on the face of a totally new reality.

So far we have been dealing with the polarity between the so-called "this-worldly" and the "other-worldly" aspects of the gospel. It is so easy, however, to falsify the polarity with a crippling effect on the gospel. If we think of the "otherness" to which the gospel refers, it is not another world above this world, not another world coming after this world, but rather another power of reality in dimensional terms, in terms of contrast, the new and the old, between the fulfilling future and the negativities of the present. For in some way this world will be included in the continuing content of the coming world, only in a new dimension, the transfiguring and glorifying dimension of the divine life. If we do not maintain this, the gospel would mean the sheer dismissal of the world that now exists; it would entail an ultimate miscarriage of the creative work of God from the beginning to the end. That is the dualistic gospel of Marcion and the Gnostics, which has survived in so much preaching about heaven and the after-life. As Irenaeus and other church fathers argued, the price of such a new world is a blasphemy against the Creator *(blasphemia creatoris).* The gospel of salvation is a way of holding out hope for this world, freed of the powers and principalities that generate sin and death, for the sake of the new generation of lasting life, peace and righteousness that endures forever.

History and Existence

A second polarity also has to do with the question of "what is to be proclaimed"—the content of the gospel. Is it *history* or *existence?* Is it a special sequence of historical events or a symbol system of existential meanings? This is not the familiar question about demythologizing, for the myth in the New Testament could be used both to interpret historical events and to express existential experiences. But is the gospel history? Does it contain history? To put it more radically, is it *only* history, that is, a report of real historical occurrences that happened at a definite time and place? Or, in contrast, is it a moving mirror of symbols of human experience that can in principle happen in any time and place? Is the gospel the story of everyman, only dramatized by the story of that man, Jesus of Nazareth, like Hamlet, Job, or Jonah is the story of everyman, so the historical question need not arise? If Hamlet did not ever exist, the truth of the story that bears his name would remain essentially the same. If Jonah did not exist, we can still accept the meaning of the story. Does the truth of the gospel have such an accidental linkage to the historical Jesus, or is the real *history* of Jesus, what he did and what happened to him in the resurrection, the very core of the gospel?

That poses the question about the historical pole of the gospel! But what about the existential? If the gospel is history, is it not history of a peculiar kind? Is it not history written from a peculiar existential perspective, an odd sort of *blik,* and very definitely linked to the apostolic interpretation of what God was deciding in the historical Jesus? Does not the gospel therefore also relate to a new understanding of existence, giving birth and expression to it? In other words, can the history *in* the gospel be interpreted *as* a wonder-full thing apart from faith and the insight granted by the Spirit of God? Does it not take a miracle of the mind to grasp the meaning of the history that happened in the person of Jesus? So is there not after all an existential dimension written into the structure of the gospel as history, not merely history as past history, but also as the preactualization of the final future of humanity in Jesus Christ? This is the re-eschatologizing of history. There is both particular history, then, and existential symbolism in the gospel to be preached. We can stand before the figure of Jesus and say "Ecce homo!" because he incorporates the essential future and truth of the humanity of each one of us and of all mankind.

Ministry as Institution or Instrument

The ministry of the church exists to proclaim the gospel in all its fullness. But what is the basis of the ministry? Does it stem from the word of the Lord? Is it a *dominical institution* or is it an *ecclesiastical instrument?* The New Testament discussions about ministry can be seen as polarized between these two views —the institutional versus the instrumental view of the ministry. Those who hold to the institutional view, if we can generalize, tend to have a so-called high-church view of the ministry; those who teach an instrumental view are holding a low-church view.

The functional theory of the ministry tends to relativize the difference between clergy and laity, perhaps even obliterate it. Mark Gibbs and T. Ralph Morton in *God's Frozen People* state that "there is no fundamental difference in calling between an archbishop and his chauffeur, between a president and a parish minister." [1] The priesthood of all believers is appealed to as the reason to downgrade the ordained ministry within the church. The theme of the general ministry of all members of the church as the "people of God" is so developed that very little room is left for a theology of special offices within the church. The minister following this viewpoint is fond of reiterating to his people that he is no different than they are. But it is mostly rhetoric, because the differences are not so easily expelled by words.

Who is the minister? Is the minister a delegated representative of his congregation, assuming functions that belong to all the people by baptismal right? If so, then one person is selected out of the many to be the minister, so that things may be done decently and in order. The result is that the ordained ministry is a matter of expediency. Practically, this means that the minister's authority derives from the will of the people; it is a more or less democratic notion. If the people do not like what they hear, they can elect another representative. "He who pays the piper calls the tune." It is a modern-day question. What is the ultimate basis of the minister's identity *qua* minister? If the catholic institutional view is correct, then the ordained ministry was instituted by Christ and its validity is transmitted by a succession of officeholders. Then the minister does not derive his authority from *below,* from the congregation which he serves, but from *above,* from the Lord of the church whose will is represented by those whom he has appointed.

Luther himself was perhaps never clear on the ultimate authorization of ordained ministry. At least Luther scholars still dispute the matter. Luther can be quoted as saying that the ministry is committed to one person, "otherwise, what would happen if everyone would speak?" It would result in chaos, Luther said, like the chatter of housewives on their way to the market, all talking at once and nobody listening. Likewise, if many hands are doing the baptism, the baby will drown. We need ministers, it would seem, purely for practical reasons. On the other hand, Luther could justify a special ministry in the church with the simple words, "Christ instituted it." It has the express command of Christ. Luther writes, "I say that according to the institution of Christ and the Apostles each town ought to have a pastor or bishop." [2] Christ ordained that some, not all, should be called for the purpose of proclaiming publicly the gospel. "As he has bound the Holy Spirit to the Word, so he has bound the proclamation of the Word to the institution of the ministry." [3] A radical laicism is hardly compatible with these words.

Luther's inconsistency can be understood in a constructive way. He offers no full-blown doctrine of the ministry, but he was operating with some instincts to which one might give expression in a more comprehensive view. Against the Roman Catholic side he could argue that if the bishops will not support the evangelical reformation of the church, the gospel was too important an issue to leave in their hands. Therefore, in an emergency situation each group of Christians could choose one from their own ranks to publicly proclaim the gospel, without episcopal ordination. However, on the other hand, he could counter the left-wing spiritualists who placed so much stress on the direct, inner call of the Spirit, by throwing his weight behind the idea of the ministry's transmission through a succession of ordained pastors.

Paul Tillich's language about "catholic substance" and "protestant principle" designates well the two poles in the ongoing ecumenical debate on ministry. Perhaps also Ernst Käsemann's thesis about "early catholicism" in the pastoral epistles versus Paul's charismatic view of ministry can provide some terms for another formulation of the same polarity. When the Spirit is breaking out all over, you can best stamp out the fire by tying the Spirit to the ecclesiastical office, subjecting all its holders to proper schooling, ordination and episcopal regulation. One hardly expects one's bishop to speak in tongues, nor a theological professor for that matter. There is no better way to control the *charismata* of the ministry than to require each ordained person to pass a test administered by both bishop and professor. In a pastoral letter of 1964 Bishop Pike was complaining about all the protocol attached to proper orders in his own Episcopalian tradition. He quipped that while Episcopalians are enjoying apostolic *succession,* other churches are having the apostolic *success.* As we hear about the flames of the Pentecostal fire spreading through parts of South America, we can not help but wonder about how closely the Spirit and the Word are bound to the office of the ordained ministry.

Individual vs. Social Salvation

A fourth polarity deals with the *individual* and the *group,* with individual versus social salvation. Is the gospel a message of personal salvation? We know that at least in the Old Testament God was dealing with a people. Does salvation then become a free-for-all in the New Testament, with each individual standing alone and on his own before God? It is doubtful that the New Testament can be read rightly from the perspective of such a highly individualistic concept of personal identity and meaning. Krister Stendahl once criticized the "introspective conscience of the West" which brought about a great stress on the application of the gospel to inner life, personal subjectivity, the anxiety-ridden soul, private confessions, etc. In recent theology there has been a strong criticism of the privatizing of the gospel, restricting it to purely personal concerns and interior spirituality, while neglecting its relevance to the public issues. Hence, the social gospel of yesterday has been succeeded by the political gospel of today, so that it might appear that Marxism is to the public side of the gospel what Christianity is to its private side. Not surprisingly the phenomenon of Christian Marxism has arisen first in our time; it is a good criticism of a ministry that became the tool of the cultured people and the ruling classes. In Europe and in America middle-class Christianity has been severely criticized, because its ministries did not make contact with the plight of workers and the ghetto-dwellers. The image of Jesus as the minister who cared for little people left out of the social contract, people barely hanging on to the edge of life, has challenged the ministry to do likewise.

Attention to the sociology of salvation is a corrective to an overly individualized gospel. However, it would be a mistake to lose the individual in the social lump. Adolf von Harnack summarized the teaching of Jesus unforgettably in terms of the infinite value of the individual soul. The gospel is great enough to care both for the whole group and for each individual. This is where the Christian gospel is infinitely superior to Marxism. The definition of an individual's worth can never be exhausted by his role in society or by his contribution to the state. Nor does a person wish to be merely a useful tool or building block on the way to the great collective utopia of the future. No state is worthy of any person's loyalty that does not care for every person's welfare. The gospel is certainly a message of personal salvation. It holds out a promise of fulfillment that answers to the deeply personal longing to be somebody, to be an individual person, to be free, to be free just to be.

But every individual is also a member of a group. The communal dimension of his existence is part of himself. The minister who cares for the individual must help create a community in which individuals become persons, friends and members one of another, to overcome the suffering of solitariness, loneliness and isolation. So the "Who am I" question, so much in vogue today, is augmented by the "Who Are We" question, and the story of one's own individual life blends into the tribal history of a people whose memories become ours, whose promises declare the fulfillment for which we all hope. Nothing is more cruel than to let a person writhe in the anxiety about his own identity without granting him a word that bestows a new identity in community with the people of Jesus Christ.

Church and World

The fifth polarity has to do with the field of ministry. Is it the *church* or the *world?* If we say both, we could mean it in the trivial sense that the minister goes into the world to preach the gospel, to make converts, and to lead the new recruits back into the church. The question is whether the minister is a man of his religious community or of the wider human community as well. Traditionally we have said, he is a minister of his community but only a citizen—like every other citizen—in the wider human community. That means, without clerical collar. Few things have irritated the laity more than to see their minister in the streets protesting with the kids or in a civil rights demonstration, or what have you. Whether the cause has to do with the thunder on the right or the conspiracy on the left, the issue is the same. Does the minister as minister of the gospel of Jesus Christ become a little Moses to help lead the human community out of bondage? Is the minister a man of the church, serving only its needs as preacher, teacher and counsellor, or is he also a man of the kingdom whose field is the world, and whose actions in the world are signs of the universal meaning of the gospel, of its power to bring hope to all men and to liberate those who are captive? Does the ministry have responsibility for the world, or is that left to politicians, educators, businessmen, labor leaders, and the like? Was a Father Groppi doing the work of the ministry, or a Father Dubi as a leader in Citizens Action Project, or the Berrigan priests in opposing the war or a Jesse Jackson in PUSH or a Camillo Torres with his revolutionary cadre? If someone says, but we must draw the line somewhere: where is that? Can one draw a clear line where the church leaves off and the world begins? Can one draw a line so as to include all kinds of functions approved by the establishment, like running for congress, teaching at a university, running a pension fund, being a college president, but then exclude all subversive, illegal, conspiratorial or revolutionary activities, no matter how justifiable in a moral sense?

In the Reformation tradition the office of the ministry is tied to the preaching of the Word and the administration of the sacraments. In fact, however, hundreds of ministers retain their ministerial status without doing either of those things. The definition of a minister is rather elastic, until he becomes con-

spicuously involved in movements of dissent, protest, or liberation in behalf of the poor and the oppressed. If the minister is
to stick to spiritual things, is not the lack of bread a spiritual
problem? Does there not exist such a network of personal and
social relations, that a ministry assigned to but a few facets of
religious experience is something less than representative of the
gospel of the universal kingdom which Jesus preached and
manifested in his own life? Do not the contents of the final
kingdom, symbolized by righteousness, shalom and love, already
achieve partial realizations, perhaps we could say sacramental
anticipations, in the everyday world in which human beings
struggle for freedom, peace and justice, for acceptance, happiness and fulfillment? These are essential dynamics and aims of
the kingdom of God that cannot be confined to the empirical
church.

The Christian minister is not like a congressman who represents the interests of his constituency. Rather, he represents the
gospel of the kingdom of God which embraces the well-being
and the future being of the world as well as of the church.
If the church calls a minister to be its servant, it cannot own
the minister. Instead, the minister is on loan to the church by
the gospel of the kingdom of God which reaches beyond the
church to include the welfare and destiny of the whole world.

The minister is a man of the kingdom; therefore he exists for
the world and against the church; he exists for the church and
against the world. He represents a twofold message of law and
gospel which has a dialectical relation to both the church and
the world. If the minister feels the squeeze of this double orientation, if he feels like a schizophrenic, that may be a good sign
that he is no mere flunkie of the institutional church that pays
his salary, that the gospel he proclaims is not an ideology used
to rationalize in sacred symbols the self-interests of his own
group and his privileged status in that group.

The Gospel of the Kingdom of God

The five basic polarities we have discussed hinge on a special
way of relating the church to the kingdom of God, the kingdom of God to the world, and the world to the church. It is, of
course, widely acknowledged that for the New Testament the

church is an eschatological event. The church as the new people of God has been founded by the eschatological event of salvation—the living, serving, suffering, dying, and rising of Jesus Christ. The church has been gathered from out of the nations in order to be constituted as a people with an eschatological mission to the world. The primary task of the church, then, is to proclaim the coming of God's kingdom as the final future of the world on the model of its advent in the ministry of Jesus Christ. The church's concern for the world derives from the fact that the kingdom of God which it represents encompasses the future of the world as well as the church. The promises of the kingdom are not for the church alone; they enshrine the hope of all the nations.

If the church at any period of her history must brace herself in opposition to the world, this is a posture which can only be justified in light of her mission to the world, and must not become a permanent state of mind. On the other hand, when the relations of the church to the world are harmonious, the church must ask whether this is a peace which has been achieved by conforming to the world. A period of smooth relations with the world might call for a revolutionary initiative by the church to become the protagonist of those who have no voice in society, and thus fulfill her role as the fighting agent of God's rule in history. The church can neither separate herself from the world nor merge with it, because then she would lose her distinctive function to keep the fires of hope burning in history for the fulfillment of individuals, of humanity and of all reality in the absolute future of God. Because the church exists to serve the kingdom of God in history, she is pointed towards the world, as light to the nations, as the new mankind foreshadowing the future of all humanity in Jesus Christ—the Omega Point. The fidelity of the church to her Lord is expressed in her vital consciousness of bearing the good news of hopeful destiny and ultimate fulfillment to the world. Any dimming of this eschatological consciousness results in a relaxation of the church's evangelical and missionary vocation in the world.

The eschatological horizon of the church, embracing the whole world, is what keeps her from identifying herself with the kingdom of God, turning in upon herself in spiritual egocentricity. The church is not the kingdom of God, but only the provisional form in which the kingdom of God is manifest in history. When the kingdom of God has fully come and the world has reached its transcendent destiny in God's own future, there will be no church. The church, however, exists now as the chosen instrument of God's rule for the sake of the world. If the church understands herself as God's eschatological mission for the world, she will not think of herself merely as a group of religious individuals who withdraw from the world to satisfy each other's emotional needs. People need emotional crutches, but it is not the church's primary business to provide them.

The failure to strike the proper balance between these three poles of the gospel—the kingdom of God, the church, and the world—will invariably result in a onesided gospel and a sectarian church. If the gospel becomes mono-polar and revolves around only one of these terms, you have the making of a beautiful sect.

Ecclesiocentricity

Let us take first the reduction of the gospel to the church. Such a reduction means that the church has become its own Lord, by building institutionally and dogmatically the guarantee of its own identity into self. We can call this ecclesiocentricity, analagous to egocentricity. Luther confronted such an ecclesiastical institution. It controlled the means of grace and thereby the destiny of the souls of men. The Roman party was sectarian, because it cramped the catholicity into an Italian mold.

The most common form of the reduction of the gospel to the church in our day is bureaucratic Christianity. The church runs by self-studies and future planning—looking into the mirror of its own bureaucratic functions and structures, trying to become the fairest of them all. Or to change the metaphor, the church is made of wheels, but unlike the wheels of Ezekiel which run by faith and the grace of God, here we have the little wheels spinning around the big wheels. This ecclesiastical reductionism happens too when the church tries to live at the expense of the world, or when she acts as though the kingdom will come by more people joining the church, or when she uses the world as a stepping stone to a higher throne among the powers of this world. This muscular picture of the church is a hangover from her sectarian past. The struggle for the preaching of the gospel in all its fullness and purity is waged against this puffed up church, the church of the grand inquisitor, the church of power and worldly wealth. It is a struggle for the humility of the church, for the poverty of the church, for the poverty of a penitent and pilgrim people. In Luther's struggle against this reductionism, he said, "How come Christ travelled on foot, but the pope in a palanquin with a retinue of three or four thousand mule drivers; how come Christ washed the feet of sinners but the Pope has them kiss his toes?"

Secular Christianity

The second mono-polar fallacy leads to another kind of sectarianism—the reduction of the gospel to the world and its enlightenment. This is particularly evident in the various versions of secular Christianity in our day. Luther encountered it in the form of humanism, embodied in Erasmus. Luther at times feared that Erasmus of Rotterdam, the leading humanist luminary of his day, was afflicted by a greater misunderstanding of the gospel than his Roman opponents. Luther would heat things up; Erasmus kept things cool, never going beyond room temperature. But Luther felt the humanistic embrace might well be the kiss of death.

There is a struggle in our day for the fullness and purity of the gospel in the polarizing of so-called liberals and progressives in all the main churches. This polarizing is going on between two types of sectarians. Since Vatican II it has been going on between the conservatives or restorationists, on the one side, who want to turn back the clock, who are clinging to the past, who stick for dear life to the Latin forms in church organization, cult and doctrine; on the other side are the secularizers, sometimes called progressives, who are so exhilarated by the novelties of the modern world that they become imitators of every wind of doctrine and fabulous fad, not taking their time to make everything captive to Jesus Christ as Lord of life and doctrine. If the conservatives have their heads screwed on backwards, the secular Christians are swallowing up everything that comes in cellophane wrapping.

We should take a lesson from Luther's style by which he refused to identify the fortunes of the gospel with the position of the Romanists or the humanists. It was by the little word *sola* that he was able to demonstrate that these two sectarianisms—

these fundamentalists and these modernists—are secretly joined to each other. They are kissing cousins feuding with each other. They are both exposed by the *sola* of the gospel—*sola gratia, sola fide, solus Christus, sola scriptura.* The purpose of the word "alone" was to reveal the sectarian character of those who make the gospel captive to the church or to the modern world.

In light of the *sola* character of the gospel, what we have witnessed as secular Christianity is a dis-grace. Literally a dis-grace, because it wants to go it alone without grace. The Christian is asked to be just a good secular man, celebrating the world come of age, as though it has been cleared of demons by the lights of science and technology; so here we have the church striking the silly pose of drooling at the world like an idiot, a world which has its own glories, to be sure, but is still doubled over with cramps in fear and anxiety about its future.

Utopianism

The failure to maintain these tri-polar relations of the gospel in terms of the kingdom of God, the church, and the world results, in the third place, to a reduction of the gospel to a future kingdom. The secular version of this is revolutionary utopianism, where the children of today are slaughtered on the altar of tomorrow, where men worship the Moloch of an illusory future, making burned offerings in the form of bullets and bombs that kill and maim people today. It is instructive for us that Luther had to fight on this front too. There was a group of religious enthusiasts who had legitimate concerns. They looked for a radical kingdom of the poor, the peasantry, the proletariat of that time. Far be it from me to say that Luther is to be exonerated for calling upon the princes to slaughter the peasants, who had every right to dream of a better world to come. But whatever the right or wrong on both sides, there was a struggle for the identity of the gospel and its way of announcing the kingdom of God. Is the gospel an enthusiasm that gives a person wings to leave the present and to live in the future? The gospel does not take sides with the future against the present; it does not call us to forget the present and to join the future. Since the Reformation, Christianity has spawned scores of tiny eschatological sects, whose lot in life was so miserable, all they could think about was jumping into the clouds and going to heaven, getting themselves translated into another world.

The gospel of the kingdom of God is not about a kingdom in the future, which makes us write off this world as a hopeless cause; it is rather about the future of the kingdom that presses itself into history, in the person of Christ first, and then in those incorporated into his love, into his freedom, his peace and the fullness of his life. It is the future of reality revealed in Christ and now really present where the living Word is preached and the sacraments are administered, as signs of the new reality that the world also is created to enjoy. Christ is not our private thing; the gospel is not our personal philosophy. The gospel of Christ is the forward thrust of the kingdom of God that arrives with power to justify the world, to make it righteous, to bring it home to its happier future in God. The eschatological enthusiasts did not use the power of the future to care for this world, but instead as an excuse to ignore it, or just blast it to hell.

Summary

We have dealt with five polarities of the gospel ministry, and then we have shown how these polarities can be maintained within the horizon of the eschatological nature of the gospel which the church has to proclaim to the world, the failure to do so resulting in serious mono-polar reductions of the gospel, in turn leading to three different types of sectarianism. The first polarity dealt with the ultimate dimension of the gospel and its universal scope, embracing and illuminating all things of a penultimate character, that is, the other-worldly and this-worldly, the transcendent and immanent poles of the Christian gospel. The second polarity of the gospel comprises the history in the kerygma as well as its existential correlative. The historical particularity of the gospel links the salvation of mankind to the story of Jesus of Nazareth. The existential relevance is based on personal participation in this event which makes it a reality for me. In the language of Sören Kierkegaard, this is to hold fast what is objectively uncertain in terms of infinite, personal, passionate interest. Thirdly, we looked at the question of the foundation of the gospel ministry, whether it stems from an institute of Christ himself or whether it evolved as an instrument of the self-institutionalizing church, whether there are grounds for preferring a more Catholic perspective on the ministry as a special priesthood over a Protestant functionalist view which relativizes and ultimately obliterates the difference between clergy and laity. A full doctrine of the ecclesiastical office would carry us into the debate on episcopacy and papacy, whether either or both happen to be of the essence of the church and therefore criteria of a valid ministry, or whether they may only have been once useful, but now obsolete elements of an authoritarian structure of the church. Fourthly, there is the polarity of the individual and the community in which one is a participating member. Is the ministry dealing with an aggregate of individuals who join to have their individual needs and interests more efficiently served, or are they members of one body, so that the meaning of their individual identity is mediated by their involvement in the group's identity? Fifthly, the ministry of the gospel can be seen as a spearhead of the kingdom of God, which moves through both the church and the world, so that there are signs of the kingdom not only in the church's sacraments but also in the world's struggles for brotherhood, equality and freedom. The minister must not only interpret the words of the past deposited in the sacred tradition, but also the signs of the times, so that the world may come to a new knowledge of itself as that has been revealed in the story of Jesus and his gospel.

With the understanding of the church, its word and ministry, that is here proposed in the light of eschatology, we can be better armed to understand the sectarianizing impulses abroad in the land, three reductions of the gospel, three ways to make a sect. The one leads to ecclesiocentricity (church-centered thinking), which is what is happening in many churches today; another leads to secular humanism (man-centered thinking) which generates the jaded optimism of so-called radical theology, secular Christianity and the God-Is-Dead movement; and thirdly, there is a revival of enthusiasm, *Schwärmerei*, taking the form of utopian or other-worldly futurism, assuming a more social this-worldly form in the commune movement and a more individualistic other-worldly form in the Jesus movement.

All of this leaves us with a flickering hope that we might again be satisfied with the gospel, with a renewal of the movement of the gospel as it came to expression in Jesus and the apostolic kerygma. That should be sufficient; that is the *satis est* to which Luther once called the church. In that we have the ground and source of the peace and humor of life under the rule of God; in that we have the formulation of the conditions of the righteousness and love that became burning bright in the cross of Jesus; in that we invest our hope for the wholeness and fullness of reality that eventually will be flooded by the glory of God. The good news of the kingdom in Jesus can create, will create, perhaps even now is creating, a movement of new vitalities coursing through the varicose veins of a church with tired blood. Where the gospel of Jesus Christ is preached, there is the church; our sectarianisms can fade away, and we will then awaken to a new and better day.

6

The Apostolic
Ministry in
the Church

It has become hackneyed to talk about the crisis of the ministry. There was an outpouring of books and articles on the
renewal of the ministry during the sixties, calling for changing
styles and new forms. But there is no clear image of the ministry at this time. Who is the minister and what is he supposed
to do? It is not even clear what kind of answer to these questions
is expected. A psychological answer? A sociological answer? A
theological answer? And what would that be? A book that is
much talked about these days is Dean M. Kelley's *Why Conservative Churches Are Growing*.[1] A minister armed with the assumptions and findings of this book will shape his ministry in
a particular way. There he will learn that a strong church is a
serious one; and the more serious the more strict. Churches
whose ministries are unreasonable, intolerant, dogmatic, segre-
gated, anti-ecumenical and other-worldly are growing; those
which try to be relevant, reciprocal, dialogical, up-to-date and
ecumenical are fast losing members. The message is that the
liberals are losing and the conservatives are winning. The book
is almost saying that the only way for your ministry to have a
future is to stand pat and resist change. Those who called for
vast changes in the ministry were surely also concerned about its
future, but they succeeded only in hastening its demise. Making
the ministry relevant to modern man, involved in the world and
theologically up-to-date, has apparently only thrown it into the
greatest confusion, and the very churches that went along with
this program of modernization—*aggiornamento* in the Roman
Catholic Church—are now reaping what they have sown.
    When we are torn between rival counsels about ministry
today, the one side pushing the minister into the world, the

other side pulling him back into the congregation, the one side embroiling the ministry in the day's social and political questions, the other side confining it to the altar and the church office, then we have to get down to basics. Then we have to get down to the root of a theological concept of the ministry whose essence outlasts the changes that are currently taking place, whose functions are constant amidst a flurry of variables.

A Theological Model of Ministry

Our ministry is the ministry of Jesus Christ that we have received on the model of the apostolic ministry. The simplest New Testament expression for this transaction is the saying of Jesus to his disciples in Luke 10:16: "He who hears you hears me." The ministry of the church today can not set its own goals and establish new *desiderata*. In essence it is concerned only that the true voice of the gospel be heard, because he who hears the gospel as the apostles preached it hears Christ himself, who is the eschatological Word of God to all men. Here we have the norm of ministry; but it can take many forms. We shall deal with them later, after establishing the normative basis of ministry in the apostolic model, which in turn looked back to the ministry of Jesus.

The question which confronted the early church, and which is still with us today is: how can this community of believers remain apostolic after the apostles have all died out? Initially the church received its identity from the living witness of the apostles to Jesus of Nazareth, his life, death and resurrection. Where this witness was absent, there could be no faith in Jesus of Nazareth as the definitive eschatological act of God and there could be no community gathering in his name, to praise God and celebrate the presence of salvation. The church was built upon the foundation of the apostolic ministry and witness to Jesus of Nazareth, "for no other foundation can any one lay than that which is laid, which is Jesus Christ" (1 Cor. 3:11).

The early church improvised answers to the question of how to keep the church apostolic in post-apostolic times. The first answer was to write things down and to make a collection of the best of them. In this way the principle of canonicity became the mark of the church's continuing apostolic character. Authentic apostolic traditions were preserved in written gospels and epistles. Secondly, baptismal and ordinational confessions were developed, and these became the embryo of the apostolic creed. Thus we have the canonic and the credal principles to assure continuity of apostolic witness in post-apostolic times. Anyone who opposes these developments in principle must have a bizarre sense of the way in which Christian faith retains its identity through the course of historical development. In addition to canon and creed, there is a cultic pattern that the apostolic church passed on. The core of this cult is sacramental, reducing to baptism, eucharist and worship. Through these media—canon, creed and cult—the apostolic faith was transmitted to post-apostolic times, not in changeless forms, but in a way which allowed an ongoing relation to the originating ground and content of faith in Jesus Christ.

So far we can expect widespread agreement among historical scholars who investigate the origins and early developments of Christianity. The rub comes when we raise the question of a special ordained ministry and its apostolic grounding and legitimation. I am not convinced that a good case can be made for such a special ministry in the church going back to the explicit teaching of the historical Jesus. The ordained ministry was not instituted by Jesus. But this is no reason to take up a negative attitude toward such a ministry. Neither did Jesus have anything to do with the development of canon, creed and cult. These were, as we have said, creations of the apostolic church in order to provide vehicles of the apostolic witness in post-apostolic Christianity. Now, I believe the same thing can be said for the phenomenon which New Testament scholarship calls "early catholicism." In this development we have the beginnings of the ordained ministry as we know it now. The church could not get along with purely charismatic ministries; a process of institutionalization was bound to enter in sooner or later. The church in history can not rely exclusively on the ministries of the charismatics. In their enthusiasms, they care little about such down-to-earth things as canon, creed and cult. It is true today, too, that the charismatics care very little about biblical, confessional and liturgical norms and how they keep the church in touch with its apostolic origins.

We have come to the point where the case must be made for a special ordained ministry in the church. Basically, it is a matter of leadership in the church for the sake of its continuity with the witness of the apostles to Jesus Christ. Could we get along without ministers? Should not every Christian be a minister? Do we not believe in the universal priesthood of all believers? Is there any justification for a special class of Christians in an order by themselves? Are we not all laity? Are not all priests? The answer is yes, but we still need leaders! The doctrine of a special ministry, up to and including the episcopacy and papacy, must never be so over-developed that we forget what it is all about. It has no other justification than to lead the church into a fuller realization of continuity with its own apostolic foundations. The ordained minister participates in the reality of the church like every other believer; but he is called to be a leader of the community, not as an official, master, ruler, hierarch, or boss, but simply as a servant performing functions that flow from the fullness of the gospel.

There has never existed a human community that could survive without leadership. It is no different in the Christian community. Whether Christ instituted a special ministry of leadership in the church or not, it was bound to arise. But such a ministry is not autonomous; it cannot speak on its own authority; it is radically subordinate to the cause of Jesus and the gospel which the apostles proclaimed. It is clearly possible for duly called and ordained ministers of the church, including bishops and popes, to become enemies of the gospel and to serve the interests of the counter-Christ in history. This happens whenever leadership has the effect of disrupting the continuity of the church with its apostolic origins. The case of heresy or apostasy arises when the church leader seriously distorts or violates the canonical and credal norms which the post-apostolic community developed to retain its identity and continuity with the apostolic witness to Jesus Christ.

What then is authentic apostolic succession? Without such a thing the church as the eschatological community of Christ would die. But of what does it consist? It does not consist primarily of a succession of office-holders that are linked by an unbroken chain to Jesus and the apostles. Rather, there is a necessary succession in the substance of the gospel and its saving significance for the whole world. The succession of ordained office-holders, transmitted in an episcopal sense, is actually a sign of the continuity of the whole church with its apostolic origins. It is a *sign* and not the *reality* itself. But we should not take a docetic attitude toward the sign, as though we would be better off without it. It is a highly desirable sign, because it symbolizes the apostolicity of the church in a specially vivid way and can even be an effective missionary instrument for spreading the gospel to all nations.

Constant and Variable Forms of the Ministry

We have stated that the essence of the doctrine of the special ministry is leadership in the church for the sake of the apostolic gospel and its universal mission in history. It is not so much a question of *who* is the minister, but rather of *what* he does. There are lots of card-carrying ministers with the proper training and right credentials who are not conspicuously animated by the preaching of the apostles. There are and always have been false prophets—hirelings—in the ministry of the church. The Apology of the Augsburg Confession states: "We should forsake wicked teachers because they no longer function in the place of Christ, but are antichrists." [2] Therefore, as much as we may hold in high esteem such institutionalized values as the sacrament of ordination and the historic episcopacy, they are not central to the gospel witness of the apostles by which the church stands or falls. They are rather instituted to assist and assure the transmission of the apostolic witness to Christ through changing times and under new historical configurations. It is always a dangerous sign when the churches place the concern for valid church order higher on the ecumenical agenda than interest in the identity of the apostolic gospel of Christ. For the unity of Christians in one form of church order is hollow—be it papal, episcopal, presbyteral, congregational, or what have you— if there is no operative grasp of the power and truth of the gospel.

If we are clear about the right and irreversible sequence of historically determined phases in the doctrine of the ministry, namely, first, the ministry of Jesus Christ, which in its finished aspect is the one cornerstone of all Christian ministry, and secondly, the apostolic ministry, which by definition ends with the death of the last apostle—and is thus a once-for-all-time-to-come type of ministry for the whole church—and thirdly, the ministry of the whole church which is sent to preach the gospel to all nations, in which every Christian participates through baptism, and fourthly, the special ministry of leadership, which is marked by the "sacrament" of ordination, for the sake of retaining true succession with the apostolic gospel, then we can proceed to focus on the essential and constant functions of the ordained ministry today.

In pressing on to the permanent features of the ordained ministry, we deliberately skip over non-essential—we could say "adiaphoristic"—and variable aspects, which all too often ignite and consume our major interests and energies. Lately, one variant issue has been the ordination of women. Is there a charism of leadership in the church from which women should be excluded by the mere fact they are women? Many of our churches have said "no" but other groups are still elevating this variant into the status of an essential mark of the ordained ministry. Another variant is the question of celibacy, so much debated in Roman Catholic circles. Another has to do with full or part-time ministry in the church. In Roman Catholic circles there was the matter of "worker-priests" and with us whether to sponsor "tent-making" ministries. Similar to the question whether a ministry of leadership should be part-time or full-time is whether the commitment to ministry should be temporary—like modern marriages are getting to be—or life-long, as ordination has always implied in the Catholic tradition, with its teaching about a *character indelebilis*. Another variant feature is whether the minister need have any academic training or be properly credentialed by a system of schooling. All these are variant features, because the answer for one side or the other does not determine whether the ministry of leadership in the church successfully retains continuity with the substance of the apostolic testimonies to the good news of eschatological salvation in Jesus Christ. Therefore, we must be primarily concerned about those essential operations of ministry without which the apostolic model of ministry cannot be implemented by the church today.

A. The Ministries Within the Church

The ministry of Jesus was explicitly confined to the house of Israel. Not so with the apostles! They carried their message to the pagan world outside, not neglecting the upbuilding of those who were already inside the household of faith. For the sake of convenience we may divide this discussion of the ministry today into two parts: the ministry of the church *ad intra* and the ministry *ad extra*. Ministers need to be told that both lie within the scope of the apostolic vision of mankind in light of the one, universal message of Jesus Christ.

1. *The Ministry of Preaching.*—What really constitutes the church in its concrete existence is the preaching of the gospel according to the New Testament. Through this preaching the church enters into communion with Jesus Christ and this in turn makes possible the communion of individual Christians with one another. One hears from time to time—even in theological schools—that "preaching is not where it's at." Here we have a self-fulfilling prophecy. If not much is expected from preaching, little effort is invested. Preaching goes forward nonetheless, like a sail filled with every wind of doctrine. The French writer, Francois Mauriac, writes, "A good priest has nothing to say to me. I watch him, and that is enough for me. The liturgy is enough for me as well: it is silent sermon. The religious order that speaks best about God is that of the Benedictines, because they never go into a pulpit. . . . How sorry I am for the Protestants, whose worship is nothing but words! The holy liturgy is the only sermon that touches me and persuades me. There is not a single preacher with whom I do not find myself in disagreement by the time he has uttered three sentences." [3] There is no doubt that there is plenty of bad preaching that deserves Mauriac's indictment. But the old Latin saying is then in order: *abusus non tollit usum.* We are not exonerated from the duty to preach because of unfaithful preachers. Jesus said to the apostles: Go, preach the gospel to all men. The day that is rescinded, the church will fade away into cultural oblivion. For the gospel is two things at the same time; it is a living word of promise that pierces and penetrates the hearts of people today— Luther called it an "acoustical event"—and it frames a story of salvation happening in the career of a person—Jesus of Nazareth. A recent book by my friend and collaborator, Robert W. Jenson, carries these two major terms in its title, *Story and Promise,* and its sub-title is even more descriptive, "A Brief Theology of the Gospel About Jesus." [4] Anyone who reads this book will be challenged by a theology which re-invests preaching with the significance it possessed in the apostolic church.

Admittedly, even when one has taken the promises to heart and has learned to tell the story straight, preaching is confronted by a special problem of language today. We are living in a time of "counterfeit language," as Martin Heidegger calls it. Inauthentic speech floods the air waves. Big business is lying, and lying has become big business. Language has become loud and ludicrous; shouting obscenities and absurdities is justified as a strategy to recover authenticity in an insane society. On the other side, language has degenerated into the objectifying functions of a technical society which can successfully manipulate and profitably control human behavior. Preaching has the incredible task of liberating language, of overcoming the credibility gap in our society between word and reality. The particular school of theology (the so-called "new hermeneutics" of Gerhard Ebeling and Ernst Fuchs) that refers to Jesus of Nazareth as the word-event is on the right track. He is the personal event in which the word is true, truly liberating and unburdening people who are victims of lies, labels, deceit, false witness, propaganda, prejudice, name-calling, misleading advertising and the like. The problem of preaching is doubly difficult in that neither preaching nor theology—its defense attorney—are trusted with the truth. Masses of people are inclined to believe with Ludwig Feuerbach that in preaching we are projecting the wishes of people into the empty sky, or with Karl Marx that preaching is the sacred ideology of the ruling establishment, to keep the underclass satisfied by dreams of another world filled with good things denied to them in this life.

In the movie *Sounder* there is a scene where the black preacher visits the wife and children of a black sharecropper who has just been condemned to two years of hard labor for stealing a chicken from a white man. I saw the movie in a downtown Chicago theater; the audience was predominantly black. The moment the preacher opened his mouth, trying to find some words of consolation, enjoining "patience in tribulation," the audience made clear from its hissing that it saw the preacher playing the exact role that Feuerbach and especially Marx assigned to him. Here preaching is neither truth nor therapy; it is illusion and mystification. It is not only hard core Marxists who see preaching in this light; I believe it is the common opinion of masses of people, perhaps even the unconscious suspicion of most in our church. I also believe that a lot of the right wing zeal and law-and-order support for religion in our society provides the Marxist hypothesis with its best evidence.

Christianity is a religion that has become a political tool of the conservatives who say that religion has nothing to do with politics; it has become an economic philosophy for those who wish to fight communism with it. The danger is that preaching will become culturally trapped and locked into the self-interests of those who run things. But one mark of the truth of preaching is that it brings power and hope also to those who have nothing to run, perhaps can't even run their own lives.

2. *The Ministry of Leading the Worship.*—If preaching the Word is telling the story of how the kingdom of God has become personal in Jesus, then administering the sacraments is the event through which that same kingdom becomes communal among the people who gather in his name, to give thanks for his presence and to celebrate his coming to the world. Along with preaching the Word, the most important thing the minister can do is to lead his people in the worship of Jesus' Father. It is through Word and sacrament that the members of the body of Christ are animated by the Spirit of the Father and his Son. The liturgy is the life-situation in which the concerns of the present, the memories of the past and the hopes of the future commingle in a creative way. The historical record indicates that the Christian faith cannot survive outside the context of worship.

The hardest thing a contemporary believer can endure is to hold so high a doctrine of Word and sacraments and attend the congregations that disgrace it. One's commitment to the church exists in full view of the contradiction between the *spes* and the *res.* Belief in the church becomes radically objective; it becomes the "substance of things hoped for, the evidence of things unseen." We believe in the church, not because of what it is but on account of its calling in the scheme of things.

Why is worship an ecclesiological constant, an essential condition for retaining continuity with the apostolic ministry? Quite simply because in the liturgical worship of the church the history of the promise of eschatological salvation from Israel through Jesus and his apostles is dramatically recapitulated and represented so that ears can hear, eyes can see, and tongues can taste what great things God has arranged for his people. The minister is the leading actor in this theater of worship. He has a good script; he should give a stirring performance. Of course, he has a hard act to follow, since in a sense he is standing in for

Christ. So every minister doing his thing—Christ's thing—may be called the "vicar of Christ."

Something must be done to make worship dramatically more true to the script. The term "drama" means "something done." Revelation in the biblical sense is God getting things done in history. Just as we have now come to view revelation dramatically as the acts of God in the facts of history, so we must also bring our liturgy in line with this biblical view of revelation. Then, liturgy plays the role of interpretation for life. The saving facts of history always find a new setting in the hermeneutical field of worship. The facts in question are not boring blobs of inertial matter, but burning coals that give off heat and light to all who pass them on to coming generations.

The role of the minister as leader of worship is pronounced in the performance of the sacraments of baptism and holy communion. Here the drama of salvation should be acted out with full use of the power of the symbolism inherent in these sacramental actions. Take baptism, for instance. The symbolism ought to bespeak a person's dying and rising with Christ. But what we usually see, instead, is a reduction of symbolism to almost invisible gestures. Immersion was once the common practice in the church. Whatever the practical reasons for having discontinued it, we should recover the practice of immersion, not because that would make baptism more efficacious, but because it might release more of the symbolic power of the ritual. A few drops of sprinkling do not make the same impact on the senses as, say, going under over your head. Some of the sects make more sense of the sacraments, even when their doctrines are abysmally deficient.

Holy communion is also action-oriented. Words are not enough. Jesus said, "This do in remembrance of me." Here we are not merely rehearsing the past. It is not the case of an unforgettable past clinging to the memories of a few traditionalists in the present. It is that unique past in which the power of the eschatological future of God exploded in history, in the person of Jesus of Nazareth, becoming proleptically present in parabolic word and paradigmatic deed. In liturgy we have hold of hot wires plugged into God's own future and, therefore, our final fulfillment. Hopes should be running high, as we share a communion meal that is a foretaste of the heavenly banquet with Christ its gracious host in the coming world. The atmosphere of the Upper Room should also be recaptured, as it relates to the cross of Christ, in which the suffering of humanity is directly taken up into the pain of God and his redemptive love.

Many a modern minister has somehow gotten the impression that he could better spend his time doing social work or playing with politics. He is himself bored with the liturgy; he lusts for the action elsewhere. Perhaps he has been mis-led by theologians for whom liturgy has never enshrined dimensions of transcendence, mystery and ecstasy. To them liturgy appears to convey the image of an introverted church infatuated with itself. Almost every theology in the modern world that has recently captured the headlines for itself has done so by virtue of a new methodism to make the church and its message relevant to the modern world. One reason these theologies have come and gone so fast is that their recipe of relevance is determined solely by the shifting moods of the times. If one looks to feelings and moods, then a case can be made for the irrelevance of worship. But if one listens to the apostolic gospel of Jesus Christ, then the liturgy defines its own kind of relevance.

We are not speaking of an esoteric relevance in other-worldly terms. As Bishop Robinson wrote in *Liturgy Coming to Life,* holy communion is the "focus, the power-house . . . the 'hot spot' of the church's whole existence." [5] We cannot make the liturgy relevant to the present social, political and economic problems that speak to the conscience of humanity. We can only discover and release its relevance. Christ is active in the liturgy to drive home the gospel of God's coming kingdom. An early Christian writer grasped the peculiar economic force of holy communion, saying: "When we come together to break bread, we must break it to the hungry, to God himself in his poor sinners." [6] The social relevance of liturgy is not an appendix to the gospel; it comes directly from the apostolic model. The apostle Paul himself wrote to the Corinthians about eating and drinking damnation to themselves because the rich were ignoring the poor in their midst, keeping back food that was to be shared with the needy. These rich "bastards" had no sense of the body of Christ present in all the members.

If sharing the bread in holy communion has any meaning for life here and now, it inheres in its power to arouse the desire to feed all who are hungry. The form this desire takes may vary from time to time and place to place. It may take the form of private charity and gifts to the Red Cross, or it may mean voting for a socialist government that promises to redistribute the wealth and to eliminate poverty by changing social structures. Holy communion in the apostolic sense is implicitly an attack on a system which permits Dives the rich man to sit in sumptuous splendor with plenty to eat, giving only a few crumbs to poor Lazarus the beggar. The rich man will surely go to hell, not for not knowing true doctrine, but for excluding the poor from his community of plenty. This suggests that communion meditations should be down-to-earth and related to problems of our common social existence, and less pious sounding and mystically sonorous. The leader of the liturgy must not let believers escape into a make-believe world. The tough issues of life are brought into the liturgy, placed in juxtaposition to the thrust of Christ in the world, making him transparent to believers as the minister *takes* and *blesses* and *breaks* and *shares* the bread and wine as the true body and blood of Christ.

3. *The Ministry of Teaching.*—In the third place we take up the ministry of teaching. Modern New Testament scholarship has refined for us the basic distinction in apostolic Christianity between *kerygma and didache*. It was Martin Dibelius, cofounder with Rudolf Bultmann of the Form Critical School, who formulated the slogan: In the beginning was the kerygma. The apostle Paul said, "It pleased God by the foolishness of the *kerygma* to save them that believe" (1 Cor. 1:21). But Paul did not only preach that people might believe; he also taught that they might understand. Once faith is created, it must be nurtured. Believers must become disciples, just as once the disciples became believers. Only then could they become apostles and only then can we become ministers with a developed charism of leadership. It is of the very nature of faith to seek understanding. Anselm's slogan *fides quaerens intellectum* expresses the essential transition from *kerygma* and *leitourgia* to *didache*. True faith which responds to the gospel of Jesus Christ has within its structure the element of knowing. In the Gospel of John the verbs "to know" and "to believe" are even used interchangeably. Take knowledge out of faith and you are left with empty feeling.

Christian teaching is "the faith once for all delivered to the saints" (Jude 3). There is the tradition of the apostles which must be passed on through teaching. The eschatological event of salvation is bound up with the history of Jesus Christ; this is not something that can be pried out of a person through Socratic mid-wifery. A person is not pregnant from birth with the knowledge of Jesus Christ. Jogging his memory by a bag of tricks will not help. He has to be taught the *paradosis* as it has made its way from one generation of teachers to another. If teaching in the church should ever substitute some other agenda for this apostolic paradosis, Christianity will lose the source and substance of its identity and mission in the world.

The minister should realize that he is the prime bearer of the apostolic tradition in each congregation. He must be a rabbi. Where some other image lures the minister away from this function, his sins will be visited on the generations to come. We are in a hand-me-down situation here. If what we hand down is a weaker version of what we received, and if the next generation plays the same trick on the one that follows in its turn, then the tradition must become increasingly weaker and watered down. A friend of mine has compared ministers of the tradition to members of a bucket brigade. We have several choices. We can pass on the buckets as we get them, until they reach the end of the brigade and the fire is quenched, or we can spill the water along the way or, worse yet, we can drop the buckets.

The teaching going on in the churches today is at a low ebb. We can boast of more great books, more learned scholarship, greater access to the knowledge of our past, more sophisticated communications, incredible libraries and research facilities, but we are producing a ministry as ignorant of its heritage as any on record to date. The reason is that the three primary functions of the ministry, that we can trace back to the apostolic model of church leadership, have become greatly blurred and weakened, and largely displaced by other interests which Christianity as a consumer religion in a capitalist society has invented. H. Richard Niebuhr depicts the self-understanding of the modern minister as one who aspires to be a big wheel, a V.I.P. who is "active in many affairs, organizes many societies, advertises the increases in membership and budget achieved under his administration and, in general, manages church business as if it were akin to the activities of a chamber of commerce." [7]

If the minister suffers from a confused image of his role, it is because the norms of the apostolic model are buried in forms of ministry that bear no essential relation to the goals of the church. Why is the minister not satisfied to be a rabbi, whose noble role is to transmit the living tradition to the coming generation? This task is especially difficult because there is no single tradition. There is a plurality of traditions, some of which are mutually exclusive, even heretical. Transmitting the tradition is a critical task, for it must be done with respect for the truth. Some of the traditions the minister has received through his church are or may be erroneous, naive, misleading, prejudicial, perhaps contrary to the prior norm of the gospel as Jesus was preached to have embodied it. He should not be a mindless ideologue of his own heritage.

There is an evil spirit in Protestantism, and now it has received a measure of hospitality in Roman Catholicism, which looks on tradition as so much rubble and dead-weight. Some call it baggage, with the clear implication that it is all *excess* baggage. In eschatological theology we speak glowingly about openness to the future and new things, but not forgetting that this future has a past, and that it does not come at us *senkrecht von vorn*, as Karl Barth's *totaliter aliter* was said to come *senkrecht von oben*. We can speak of this future, the future of Christian hope, because it "rhymes with the past" in a special way, to use an expression from Jenson's book, *Story and Promise*. We learn to speak of this future and how to hope for it by the logic of the language that tells forth the promises of Jahweh and the story of Jesus, as the apostles related them. If we speak of the future of Christ as our future, it is one which has had a down-to-earth career of making new traditions. It is our job to sort out the good from the bad.

We have a rich tradition that links up with the history of Jesus Christ via the apostolic ministry. It is a tradition of faith, of language, of remembered events and moving interpretations, of liturgies and hymns and prayers, of martyr and missionary deeds, of theological works and commentaries, of creeds and confessions, etc., etc. The minister is the chief hermeneut of his traditions. He should keep in mind, as many ministers do not, that Christianity as a historical religion is always only one generation away from possible extinction. If a minister is not working hard at teaching the history of his tradition in a critical way, he is a gospel pervert.

4. *The Ministry of Counseling.*—Another form of ministry that has enjoyed a great inflation in the modern church is pas-

toral counseling. The message of the church commits it to care for the whole man in his individual personal existence. The pastoral counselor is not a second rate psychologist, but a minister of the church which has been given the keys of the kingdom, along with the charge to bind and loose. The temptation is severe for the pastor to grab any old bag of tricks that seem to do the job. Of course, the pastor is free to use what psychology can teach him, but he should not be ashamed of the unique dimension in the church's own ministry of healing. In what does that consist? The prayer of the church is a healing action among the people. The church is working hardest and may even be most relevant to the problems of people when it is in prayer. We all know to what extent the pragmatic temper has seeped into our sub-conscious minds, so that when we do pray, we are not so sure we are doing anything very relevant. If prayer has a healing component, it is because in some way it brings us near to the zone of God's free grace—the power of life and salvation.

We do not need to get into the argument whether prayer is to be called a "means of grace," a kind of third sacrament, as Gustaf Aulén does in his dogmatics. But Aulén is right in saying that prayer is not merely the human act of man turning to God; it is at the same time a divine act by which God draws people unto himself. Prayer is not only the quest of divine communion in love; it presupposes this communion and is an expression of man's being grasped by God's grace and love. If we are thanking God, we are thanking him for his grace; if we are interceding, we are interceding for his grace; when we are confessing our sin, we are receiving his grace; when we are adoring God in language of praise, we are mindful of his grace above all. Grace is at the center; grace is the power of health; grace is Christ communing with us really and forgivingly.

We cannot leave the ministry of counseling in the hands of a few trained specialists. How devastating for the life of the whole church when the lay people get the idea that if they have problems, there is only one thing to do, and that is to go to their pastor. The whole community is a royal priesthood. Each Christian is ordained a witness of Jesus Christ as the Healer and Savior. As brother counsels brother, it may happen that the most loving and necessary act is to solicit the help of persons specifically trained and endowed in the art of Christian counseling, and this in turn may lead to the technical help of secular specialists in psychotherapy and psychopathology. But this must not become a substitute for the mutual consolation of Christian brothers in the name of Christ. If the church must operate special programs, these should be seen as emergency situations, and should not cut the nerve of that universal responsibility in the community of one member for the other. A special ministry is called for in our time and place to deal with the galloping disease of mental and spiritual disintegration, but it should not become so specialized that the whole community is relieved of its share in this ministry.

B. THE MINISTRIES TO THE WORLD

When the church turns to the world, the substance of her ministry can be summarized in terms of the evangelistic word and the diaconal deed. This is, to be sure, the ministry of Christ through the whole church, but here too the church will recruit and commission or ordain those who have exhibited certain charisms of leadership.

1. *The Ministry of Evangelism.*—The task of evangelism is to tell the story of the gospel to those in whom faith cannot be presupposed. These are roughly of two kinds, first, the nominally Christian and, secondly, the outright heathen. These functions used to be distinguished in terms of "home missions" and "foreign missions." Such terminology may have now been exchanged for a better one, but whatever terms we use we must keep in mind the real situational differences.

Here in the West we are living in what many call "the post-Christian era." Teeming millions of baptized persons, bearers of the indelible mark of the cross, do not confess Christ with their lives, only curse him with their lips. Never in the history of the church have there been so many *lapsi*. Nothing as spectacular as the counter-Christ has appeared within the church, though Luther thought he saw him sitting on the papal throne. What we have rather is this flabby amorphous blob of baptized, even confirmed, persons who are now indifferent to Christ and his church. The church in the West has the staggering task of reclamation. When this function is called evangelism, there are some who understandably shudder, not least in a big campaign like Key '73. Yet this is a task which, whatever we call it, will demand special approaches and agencies, a special ministry.

We think most readily, perhaps, of the high-powered evangelists who appeal to the masses, but many people are deaf to this noise. Apologetics is a form of evangelism "to the cultured despisers of Christianity." In many ways apologetics has become one of the anemic disciplines in modern theology. Largely under the influence of Karl Barth apologetics became discredited as a pseudo-theological attempt to find human reasons for a revelation which comes directly from above. Barth accused the entire line of modern Protestant theology from Schleiermacher to Tillich as man's effort to base revelation on experience, history, or reason. So he defined revelation in totally transcendental terms, removing it from the spheres in which apologetics had moved. Karl Barth's warning has to be heard. Apologetics became the tail that wagged the dog; the specificities of the Christian faith were reduced to the bare minimum so that dogmatics as the reflection on God's Word in history languished. Nevertheless, we can be grateful to men like C. S. Lewis and Paul Tillich that they carried on the ministry of apologetics. Their writings became the threshold over which many a person has passed from skepticism into a robust Christian faith.

Besides this work of reclaiming the backsliders in the faith, there is the ministry to the heathen. Some must be commissioned today, as in the early church, and sent out by congregations to do mission work among the pagans in other cities where the gospel has not yet been preached. The Lord's command is to go out to the nations. This form of ministry is today the subject of much uncertainty among missionaries themselves. What is the goal of missions? Cultural exchange? Faithful witness? Dialog? Conversion?

There are certain components of this mission to the heathen which must be acknowledged. First, when the church goes to the heathen with the gospel, it is not adding anything to the reality of salvation. The church goes with a message of salvation, the news that Jesus Christ died and was raised not just for those who happen to believe but for all men. He died for the ungodly and sinners. The church has to announce the message of how the captives have been set free. Secondly, the mission to the heathen is the task of the whole church, not just of the few who like to go to exotic places, get undersalaried and risk their lives. Missions cannot be a hobby of the church. Thirdly, the church's mission must be careful not to be a subtle form of colonialism, and not carried out in the spirit of the holy crusades of the Middle Ages. Since what we have received as man on Christ's mission is by grace alone, there is no ground for intolerance or a superiority attitude. We do not go as the enlightened to barbarians, as if our culture, politics, economics, science and technology have to be all accepted as part of the package deal. The day in which we could get away with that sort of thing is passed. Fourthly, it follows too that the gospel must be preached in all its fullness and without compromise. Though there is a danger in syncretism, it may not prevent the indigenizing of the gospel, seeking its incarnation in existing thought forms, in the psychological and sociological structures of the land, without superimposing upon the "new church" all of the philosophical accretions of Western Christianity. The Scylla of syncretism and the Charybdis of colonialism must both be averted.

2. *The Ministry of Serving.*—Another form of ministry may be called the diaconate, after the New Testament word, *diakonia.* This term simply means a rendering of service. The term goes back to Acts 6 where seven men were selected to look after the wants of the needy, especially the widows, so that the apostles could devote themselves more to the ministry of prayer and the Word. Later in the first century the term had come to mean a regular office in congregational life, alongside of presbyters and bishops. In the history of the church the diaconate began to lose its social meaning such as helping the poor and the needy, and took on ecclesiastical liturgical meaning. The deacon became an assistant pastor in the Protestant churches, or the diaconate was the last stage prior to the priesthood in the Roman Catholic church. In the Lutheran church, although spottily, the term has referred to the social work of helping the helpless. In this sense, the term is enjoying a kind of recovery today.

But actually, in a broader sense, the church's total ministry is *diakonia.* What does the church ever do that is not *diakonia?* Her life is service. But since it is true that what is everybody's business ends up being nobody's business, the church must also do diaconate work in the more special sense. The church can be so busy tending to the needs of the healthy and regular members and of existing in contact with the upper strata of people in society, that she does not see the poor and needy lying in the shadows. Pastors, full-time lay workers in congregations, synod officials, board members, institutional functionaries, teachers in colleges and seminaries move in grooves and ride in ruts where the sick and the feeble, the refugees and orphans, the idiots and the insane never travel. They are put aside into institutions. We hire people to get these people out of our sight. So the church must have a special way of expressing its diaconate character through people who in behalf of the whole church extend the helping hand and identify physically with the least of these little ones, the *elaxistoi* that Jesus always had in mind and lived to serve. The church in our society tends to see and serve merely the affluent classes that rise to the conspicuous surface, and remains oblivious to those little ones who cling to life at the margins of society. When the Christian community does not see these burdensome creatures as brothers in Christ, she no longer sees the Christ in these brothers, the naked, hungry, thirsty, homeless, sick and imprisoned Christ. The really true and primary Deacon is Jesus Christ himself, the Good Samaritan who helps those who have fallen among thieves, and the church must go and do likewise.

The diaconate ministry is much needed today. It is from those who work at the lean fringes of society who can see things better and more prophetically than those of us who live in the fat at the center. Social criticism emanates from the circumference, from Christian people who have gone to live in the valley of lepers, in the jungles of Harlem, in the wilderness of the south side. Social criticism is needed so that the church may be driven to think and act angrily against all injustice, not only to help the victims of social disorder, but also to attack the foundations of that disorder which produces the victims. The church cannot afford to be conservative, that is, conservative of those social arrangements which are unjust, however traditional, and dehumanizing, however American. This may mean that the servant community will be crucified by the ruling political, economic, and religious powers because in championing the cause of the downtrodden and forgotten, it attacks the roots of social evil that undergird the exploitative system.

The servant will be prepared even to die. There are causes worth dying for still in our American life. One does not have to go behind the iron curtain in order to encounter the test of Christian *martyria*. The church has so little social passion because it does not see things through the eyes of the diaconate

ministry. How the church can be given the vision and the heart
of the Samaritan servant, the chief Deacon in our midst, Jesus
Christ, how it can carry out this vision and resolve in concrete
deeds where people suffer, and how an army of deacons and
deaconesses can arise in the church, these are questions upon
which the discharge of the full ministry of the church hangs in
the balance. For all the best preaching will be only sounding
brass and tinkling cymbal without the servant-love of Jesus
Christ.

7

Eschatology: The Key to Christian Ethics

The aim of this chapter is to lay hold of the roots of Christian ethics and to put them back into the ground of biblical eschatology where they belong. The argument will be advanced in four giant steps. The first step consists of a pair of observations concerning the present state of the discipline of Christian ethics, namely, that while a few contemporary ethicists acknowledge that eschatology holds the key to ethics, most of the leading names completely ignore it, especially in America. The second step proposes that the one normative starting point for Christian ethics is the eschatological kingdom of God which Jesus preached and practiced. Thirdly, eschatological ethics may be reciprocally related to philosophical ethics; it can appropriate the categories which appear in the light of philosophical analysis, and at the same time offer a comprehensive viewpoint which can overcome the contradictions that classically cling to the various types of philosophical ethics. Fourthly, a brief outline of the elements of an eschatological ethic will be presented, to exhibit the promise it holds in furthering the task of developing a more adequate theory of Christian ethics.

Eschatology as the Key to Christian Ethics

We return, then, to our first point: eschatology as the key to Christian ethics. If it is true that eschatology is the key to Christian ethics, then one must conclude that the most prominent thinkers in this field have not yet found the key. Samples of their thinking can be found in such comprehensive anthologies as those edited by Gene H. Outka and Paul Ramsey, *Norm and Context in Christian Ethics*, by H. H. Schrey and Helmut Thielicke, *Faith and Action*, by Ian T. Ramsey, *Christian Ethics and Contemporary Philosophy*, as well as the surveys by James Gustafson, in his book, *Christian Ethics and the Community*, and by Edward LeRoy Long, Jr., *A Survey of Christian Ethics*. One looks in vain for a solid discussion of eschatology and ethics in these large anthologies. They proceed as though the starting point of Christian ethics lies elsewhere, as though the debate on eschatology in the historical origins of New Testament Christianity has no fundamental significance to their discipline. Perhaps we need go no further than the following observation by James Gustafson for a sufficient explanation: "Americans have done little work in the history of Christian ethics; they have done less on the relation of ethical thought to biblical scholarship; only a few scholars have moved with ease between systematic theology and ethics." [1]

There is an explanation, however, that goes deeper than the notorious indifference of Christian ethicists to the results of biblical scholarship. Christian ethicists ignore the connection between eschatology and ethics [2] because of a prior disjunction between the two in the theological systems on which they have had to draw. Until recently systematic theology has treated eschatology as an illegitimate offspring of primitive Christianity, and therefore as something adventitious to the essence of the faith in modern times. The dogmatic prejudice against an organic tie between eschatology and ethics is therefore only a reflection of the prior neutralization of eschatology in apologetics and systematics. We can hardly expect ethics to bear fruit where no seeds of the kind have been sown by the systems of theology which they presuppose.

But who says that eschatology is or should be the key to Christian ethics? Perhaps Christian ethics is justified, after all, in ignoring the eschatological thematic. It would clearly have the weight of the tradition in its favor. In the structure of traditional theology, Roman Catholic and Protestant, eschatology dealt with the "last things" of history and an other-worldly future, whereas ethics dealt with moral problems of life in a this-worldly present. Hence, the disjunction between eschatology and ethics in contemporary ethical thought is no recent lapse; it follows the traditional pattern. Occasionally, however, one runs across hopeful pronouncements in the literature such as this one by Helmut Thielicke: "Theological ethics is eschatological or it is nothing." [3] But then Thielicke fails to pursue the matter. Paul Ramsey takes up the theme of eschatology in the ethical teachings of Jesus, but treats it as a distinct liability. So he can say that although the ethics of Jesus originated in the context of apocalyptic eschatology, we should remember "that *genesis* has nothing to do with *validity*." [4] Reinhold Niebuhr also acknowledges, but barely, that "there is, nevertheless, an eschatological element in, and even basis for, the ethics of Jesus." [5] But he too in the end forgives Jesus his eschatological trespasses, and states —astonishingly, in the light of our present knowledge of the role of the kingdom of God in the teachings of Jesus—that "the ethic of Jesus is the perfect fruit of prophetic religion." [6] It is understandable then that Reinhold Niebuhr would not welcome the new theology that calls for a reconsideration of the kingdom of God for theology and ethics today. He said, "We've been through this business of the Kingdom before." [7] He was thinking, of course, of Walter Rauschenbusch's idea of the kingdom of God and the collapse of the social gospel which Niebuhr's own criticism helped to effect.

The attempt to take up "this business of the kingdom" again is backed by the conviction that Niebuhr was wrong about the ethics of Jesus, and that we cannot so easily eliminate or de-emphasize the eschatological worldview that penetrated his message and activity in a contemporary statement of Christian faith and ethics. Christian ethics must at least consider what the implications might be if, for example, it were to take seriously a statement like this, by T. W. Manson: "We must recall the fact that the ethic of the Bible, from beginning to end is the ethic of the kingdom of God." [8] In *Eschatology and Ethics in the Teaching of Jesus,* Amos N. Wilder made a good beginning at taking seriously the ethic of Jesus as an eschatological ethic; but this book is a loner in the field and hardly rates a footnote now and then. Edward LeRoy Long's *A Survey of Christian Ethics* does not even give it a single mention. I am not saying that Wilder's book has set an example which we ought to follow; it defines eschatology in the Platonic terms of C. H. Dodd's realized eschatology, which 1 find unacceptable. But at least it focuses on a theme which still calls for more serious treatment than it has received in contemporary ethics.

The most far-reaching proposal to recall ethics to its eschatological home has been advanced by Wolfhart Pannenberg. We can call it eschatological ethics, or ethics of the kingdom of God, or just proleptic ethics. This chapter shares the view that Christian ethics must begin with the eschatological thrust of Jesus' ethics. This can lead to a complete reconstruction of the foundations of ethics. An essential connection between ethics and eschatology will be established; ethics will go back into the business of the kingdom of God, and in this way meet a New Testament standard of what is essentially Christian.

The Ethical Relevance of the Eschatological Kingdom

Pannenberg is not alone in linking ethics radically to eschatology. The central issue of eschatology and ethics, which Amos Wilder took up in the mode of realized eschatology, is now being emphasized in the works of Richard Hiers, an American New Testament theologian, who is reissuing a form of the futurist view of the kingdom held by Albert Schweitzer and Johannes Weiss. Hiers writes, "In the realm of moral theology, it needs scarcely be mentioned that the term 'kingdom of God' has now passed out of currency. Once the watchword of the Social Gospel movement, which looked for the establishment—slowly, perhaps, but surely—on earth through human moral effort, this category has given place to others, for instance, in the terminology of Reinhold Niebuhr, to 'prophetic religion.' " [9] There is no evidence that Richard Hiers is linking his exegetical work to the theological program of Wolfhart Pannenberg.[10] They have worked in complete independence of each other, but for both the idea of the future eschatological kingdom in the message of Jesus is the moving agent of his ethical teachings.

In spite of the fact that Pannenberg is placing the eschatological thematic, the kingdom of God, into the context of contemporary ethical thought that is almost totally void of interest in eschatology, he is actually not doing an unprecedented thing. Norman Metzler wrote his doctoral dissertation, *The Ethics of the Kingdom of God,* under Wolfhart Pannenberg at the University of Munich, tracing the development of the bond between the kingdom of God and ethics from Immanuel Kant, through Friedrich Schleiermacher, Richard Rothe, Albrecht Ritschl, and concluding with some of Ritschl's most important pupils. Pan-

nenberg is thus hooking up with the kingdom-of-God theology
in the nineteenth century, only under the drastically new conditions that have meanwhile prevailed in New Testament studies since the time that Johannes Weiss and Albert Schweitzer
criticized so severely the dominantly ethical concept of the kingdom of God in Ritschlian circles. It was, in fact, the severity of
Weiss's judgment that Ritschl's ethical concept of the kingdom
of God is related to Jesus' eschatological view *in name only* that
helped to bring about the sudden death of the kingdom of God
in ethics. He wrote, "As Jesus conceived of it, the kingdom of
God is a radically superworldly entity which stands in diametric
opposition to this world. That is to say that there *can* be no talk
of an *innerworldly* development of the Kingdom of God in the
mind of Jesus! On the basis of this finding, it seems to follow
that the dogmatic religious-ethical application of this idea in
more recent theology, an application which has completely
stripped away the original eschatological-apocalyptical meaning
of the idea, is unjustified. Indeed, one proceeds in an only apparently biblical manner if one uses the term in a sense different
from that of Jesus." [11] The leading post-Weissian theologies,
dialectical theology and existentialist theology, allowed the
kingdom of God to play no controlling role. The theme, however, continued to survive in isolation in the works of New
Testament exegetes—C. H. Dodd, W. G. Kümmel, J. Jeremias,
G. Lundström, T. W. Manson, Norman Perrin, and many others
—until Pannenberg found a way to give this theme a new lease
in the realm of systematic theology and ethics.

The basic proposition of this new lease is that the Weissian
critique of Ritschl's ethical concept of the kingdom of God, so
far from requiring the expulsion of the theme, provides on the
contrary the opportunity to overcome a fatal defect in Ritschl's
theology and thus to develop in a new and more adequate way
the essential bond between eschatology and ethics, pointing out
a way for Christian ethics to go in the future. The fatal flaw in
Ritschl's theology, according to the Weissian critique, is that
the kingdom of God is there brought about as a result of human
ethical activity through the progressive development of history.
It is strange to speak of the kingdom as the kingdom of *God*, if it
is subject to the cumulative and progressive results of man's
ethical actions. Günter Klein, in his recent essay on "The Biblical Understanding of 'The Kingdom of God,' " asks the rhetorical

question, "For what kind of *God's* rule is it whose coming depends on the activity of *man?*" [12]

Ritschl's idea of the kingdom of God was thus fraught with a glaring contradiction; an exchange of roles takes place in which eschatological roots are made to dangle from their ethical fruits. Eschatology as the ontological prius of ethics becomes instead its sequel. In this scheme eschatology functions as a kind of teleological process, in that the future goal of the kingdom is being realized by the present ethical achievements of mankind. In this way, a close bond between eschatology and ethics is established, to be sure, but at the expense of the priority of the eschatological kingdom of God over the ethical actions of men in the present. This is the point of Weiss's criticism of Ritschl's theology; it is also the point of departure for Pannenberg to establish the connection between the kingdom of God and ethics in a new way.[13] Weiss's negative criticism has been turned to a positive result by Pannenberg; he shows that the thoroughly eschatological character of the kingdom of God is not antithetical to ethics, but is its very source and motive. To be sure, men cannot build the kingdom of God by their hands; that would only result in a Tower of Babel. The nineteenth century doctrine of progress, and the whole ethical developmental teleological schema, has come crashing down in the twentieth century, partly because of inner-theological criticism, and partly also because of extra-theological events.

If, then, the kingdom of God is not the product of ethical activity, because as the rule of God it is already prior to and stands over against it, what is the relation of ethics to the eschatological future? The clue to the relationship of eschatology to ethics may be discovered by establishing the nature of the presence of the eschatological future in the person and activity of the historical Jesus. The key term is *proleptic;* there is a proleptic presence of the eschatological kingdom in the activity of Jesus. The kingdom of God which is really future retains its futurity in the very historical events which anticipate it in the present. Christian ethics is not to be understood as the means of producing the future kingdom of God, but only as annunciation, anticipation, and approximation, let us say as "signs of the coming kingdom." Christian ethics must be cast into the shape of eschatological christology; for as the eschatological rule of God was proleptically present in the speech and actions of Jesus, so also this same eschatological reality can embody itself in the ethical actions of Christians who allow that rule swaying power in their lives. The right order is this: first, thy kingdom come, then, thy will be done. The coming of the kingdom in its priority and power is the ground of the possibility of doing God's will on earth. Ethical actions are real, although never more than provisional representations of the ontologically prior and eschatologically future kingdom. Such ethical actions do not realize the kingdom; rather, the kingdom reveals itself through actions that prefigure its coming. The kingdom of God as the highest good may be said to be proleptically present in the ethical decisions and deeds that approximate its ultimate qualities.

The proleptic structure of eschatological ethics has a twofold edge. On the one side, the futurity of the kingdom maintains a critical distance over against the present, so that every human effort and every social form are revealed to be imperfect and tentative approximations of the future kingdom, giving no one any ground for boasting before the Lord who judges all things. On the other side, the presence of the future kingdom in proleptic form offers a real participation in its life, generating a vision of hope and the courage of action to change the present in the direction of ever more adequate approximations of the eschatological kingdom.

So far we have dealt merely with the formal relations between eschatology and ethics. The material reality of the eschatological kingdom of God that has been revealed through its proleptic presence in Jesus of Nazareth is *love*. Love is the definitive content of the eschatological future of God to which Jesus surrendered himself in absolute openness, devotion and trust. Eschatological ethics is therefore *agape* ethics; the reality of God's eschatological kingdom that came to expression in Jesus' life and ministry was the power of unconditioned love. Christian ethics of love, so much advertised in situation ethics and the new morality, is radically dependent on the ontological priority of God's eschatological love, otherwise it loses its Christian character and degenerates into the ethics of desire. This desire is to Christian love what license is to Christian liberty. One is a counterfeit of the other, close enough to fool many people.

The reality of God's love is thus the prius of the loving that people become free to do through the power of forgiveness. The right order is this: "We love because he first loved us" (1 John

4:19). It is not that the kingdom grows in the measure that people love each other. It would be both too presumptuous and too burdensome for people to build up the future kingdom of God's love through their loving actions. There is a critical distance between God's love and human love that can never be bridged from the side of man. The real aim of liberated love is not to build up the kingdom of God; it is indeed sufficient of itself. Neither God nor his kingdom are in need of man's love. Rather, it is always the other person who needs our love. It is also true that we need to love other persons just as we need to be loved by them, because love is essentially the power to unite those who belong to each other. It is restless until it wins the victory of a totally fulfilling union. In the end this is life in the fellowship of God's eternal love. Meanwhile—and that's always now— God's love is concretely at work in history, both through the actions of personal love, however imperfect they always are, and through the demands of justice, which is the form God's love takes in ordering social life.

A Philosophical Reflection on the Theological Model

With this modest beginning, we have established only two things about Christian theological ethics, first, that the one normative starting point is the priority of the eschatological kingdom of God over the ethical situation of man, and secondly, that the concrete content of that future kingdom that became proleptically present in Jesus' total ministry is love. What kind of an ethic is this, when compared to the various types of philosophical ethics? Before we give a fuller sketch of the elements of eschatological ethics, it may be profitable to identify and clarify this theological model in light of current philosophical analysis.

The work in philosphical ethics by William K. Frankena [14] provides us with the readiest help in classifying various theories of moral obligation and moral value. He boils down the age-old debates in ethics to two basic types, (1) deontology—"do your duty, do what is right for its own sake," and (2) teleology— "seek the good, do what will achieve a good end." These in turn Frankena breaks down into possible sub-types, such as act-deontology or act-teleology—"there are no rules, but get the facts straight and then decide"; rule-deontology or rule teleology— "there are principles of moral obligation that tell us what to do"; and then he invents a third sub-type, summary rule, which somehow has the flexibility of love and the concreteness of law. Summary rules are guidelines for conduct but not hard and fast laws. This sub-type has been devised to accommodate an ethics of love which wants to steer between a stiff legalism and an empty antinomianism. Now, to which of these types does an eschatological ethics of agape most closely conform? Or is it a genuinely third type altogether? Frankena himself says, "It may be that we must regard pure agapism as a third kind of normative theory in addition to deontological and teleological ones." [15] But on second thought he prefers not to open up a third type, but classifies the ethic of love as a type of teleology, for to love is to have good as the end in view. Paul Ramsey, however, vigorously objects to this treatment of agapism. With Kantian fervor he attacks teleology and instead connects agapism more closely to the deontological type. So he says, "If agapism is *not* a third and a distinctive type of normative theory which is neither *teleology* (goal-seeking) nor *deontology* (an ethics of duty), then it seems to me more true to say that it is a type of deontology than to say that it is a type of *teleology*. . . . Therefore Christian normative ethics cannot primarily be a type of teleology. It cannot derive its notion of what's right from a notion of what's good, or from goals that are worth seeking." [16]

This disagreement between Frankena and Ramsey illustrates the deep cleavage between contemporary philosophical and theological ethics. Theologians have leaned more to the deontological type, philosophers more to the teleological, i.e., to utilitarianism. Some theologians have wanted nothing to do with either, and instead create a new third type, for example, H. Richard Niebuhr's ethics of responsibility,[17] which enjoins to do what is fitting in each situation, or Anders Nygren's third type, dispositional ethics, which he identifies as the *Grundmotif* of Christian ethics.[18] One can safely agree with the philosopher, Frankena, that theologians have not yet made up their minds about how to classify their ethics of love.[19] And I must admit that I have a hard time making up my mind about this.

Perhaps to reach a decision on this we should start with the one bit of consensus we do have in theology, namely, that in any theory of moral obligation love is the uniquely prime principle, whether or not other principles are admitted subsequently. *Love is the answer to the question of what is right*—ultimately. However, if our previous line of argument is correct, we cannot build an ethics straightaway from love, for love must be understood within the horizon of the kingdom of God, as the decisive power of life released by the coming of that kingdom, as present ethical action conditioned by the priority of the eschatological future. This eschatological future reveals itself in Jesus as the highest good for which men can strive, as the fulfilling destiny of human life and the goal of the whole creation. This identification of the kingdom of God with the highest good which orients men in their ethical activity gives us the heart of the theory of moral value. *The kingdom of God is the answer to the question of what is good*—ultimately. "But seek first his kingdom and his righteousness, and all these things shall be yours as well" (Matthew 6:33).

These two questions, what is right (theory of moral obligation) and what is good (theory of moral value), are given *theological* answers in Christian ethics. This means that theology draws upon an input that is not available to philosophical ethics. Paul Lehmann has stated this difference in rather extreme fashion when he says, "Christian ethics is not concerned with *the good*, but with what I, as a believer in Jesus Christ and as a member of his church, am to do. Christian ethics, in other words, is oriented toward revelation and not toward morality." [20] Of course, I cannot accept such a disjunction between "the good" and what a Christian is "to do," nor the one between revelation and morality. But I do accept that Christian ethics has to define what is good and what is right with reference to the coupling of the kingdom of God and his creative love in the person of Jesus Christ. Thus, philosophical and theological ethics share the leading questions about what is good and what is right, but theology can ground the answers to these two questions in the unity of the eschatological rule of God's love, whereas philosophy tends to set up a competition between two sets of answers, with one school choosing to elevate one despite all of its exposed liabilities and contradictions.

From the perspective of eschatological ethics, it is not necessary to choose this day which we will serve, deontology or teleology. The decision could as well be for the one or the other. We are on the teleological track when we stress that the good which man lacks—both in his being and his doing—and for which he strives, whether he knows what to call it or not, is nothing else than the kingdom of God. I would prefer to call this an ethics of fulfillment. Paul Lehmann's favorite term is "maturity." It is similar to what I mean by the fulfilling future of man which he now lacks, and for which he longs and hopes, despite the fact that he also exists in sinful contradiction to it. But we leave the teleological track in the moment that we acknowledge that our ethical actions do not produce that fulfilling future, but at best only anticipate and express it in approximate ways. The good ends at which we aim in our ethical decisions are not in an empty space lying in the future. The function of christology in eschatological ethics is to provide a paradigm of the good, a sample of fulfillment in human existence, and therefore some definite controls in determining what goals are worth seeking and by what means. A teleological ethic leaves the definition of the end up in the air; an eschatological ethic brings it down to earth.

Thus, there is a deontological thrust as well in eschatological ethics, for deontology stresses the priority of what is right over against what is merely useful or desirable. For what is right is what God lays upon every person as an obligation—to love his neighbor as himself. It is always right to love; it is always an obligation rooted in the transcendent imperative of God's will. It is right for us to love each other, as God has loved us, whether we are able to do so or not. Whether or not we feel full of love has no bearing on the issue of obligation. The element of deontology preserves the critical distinction between the highest good to which we are essentially related and even the best ethical actions which always fall short of God's righteousness. "You, therefore, must be perfect as your heavenly Father is perfect" (Matthew 5:48). This saying retains its validity even though we concede it is existentially impossible, in this kind of world with our kind of human beings.

We have reached the messy conclusion that eschatological ethics does not fit into either of the philosophical modes, because the eschatological conditionedness of ethics puts a different light on the questions of what is right and what is good. Theological answers to these questions make assumptions about the reality and revelation of God, his saving events in history, and the proleptic manifestation of his eschatological future in the person of Jesus. The absence of such assumptions is bound to make a substantial difference. Nevertheless, philosophical analysis makes us more aware of the logic implicit in theological ethics. The ethics of fulfillment and the ethics of love are inseparable. The right thing to do is always to seek the good of our neighbor, which is to act in such a way as to open him to his greater fulfillment. Love is in the service of the other person's fulfillment. Hence, logically there is a certain priority to the question of the good. The fulfillment of humanity is the good which God promises with the coming of his kingdom. But the means that God's love creates to seek that fulfillment is a matching love. The kingdom of God is the highest good in ethics; love is the criterion of how to act in relation to the goal of attaining the greatest possible fulfillment of people. Hence, there is no way to play off love against fulfillment, or fulfillment against love, because Christian ethics goes hand in hand with both. But this does not mean that there is a third type, in addition to deontology or teleology, that could be included within a philosophical classification. I suspect that if eschatological ethics were submitted to philosophical criticism, it would be designated a mixture of deontology and teleology, resembling now one, now the other. On the other hand, if eschatological ethics turns out to be a distinctly third type, it would still be different from either of those proposed by H. R. Niebuhr and Anders Nygren. For neither of them deals with the foundations of ethics in the kingdom of God.

Eschatological Ethics in Outline

It remains now to furnish a threadbare outline of eschatological ethics, indicating where it stands on many of the debated issues.

(1) In the first place, if the prime category and organizing principle of eschatological ethics is the kingdom of God as the highest good and fulfilling future of mankind, a lot will be riding on how the reality of the kingdom of God is interpreted, whether other-worldly and future, as in the traditional orthodox interpretation, which permits no real connection between eschatology and ethics, or whether this-worldly and present, as in the existentialist demythologizing interpretation, whose eschatology is radically realized in the moment of ethical decision, or whether other-worldly and present, as in dialectical theology, which affirms the primacy of the eschatological theme for theology,[21] but

neutralizes its potential for ethics, or whether this-worldly and future, as in one wing of the new theology of hope, which talks about bringing in the kingdom of God on earth through man's technological planning and political participation, thus repeating the error we have cited in the Ritschlian school. In eschatological ethics the emphasis lies on the theocentric futurity of the kingdom—it is the truly future eschatological kingdom of God —which has achieved a present impact in the person of Jesus and wherever the word of this presence exercises its creative power. The future of the eschatological kingdom does not cease to be distinctly future in the events in which it becomes proleptically present. Therefore, it is not really a question of whether this kingdom is future or present, for there is a proleptic presence of the eschatological future, nor whether it is other-worldly or this-worldly, for the eschatological kingdom is not a future condition in history produced by the progressive and cumulative good works of mankind. Rather, the kingdom of God is the transcendent future of history which retains its ontological identity and priority in the process of determining the meanings of events in history and their moral implications. It is the kingdom of God that comes in power to determine the decisions that disclose the destinies of men.

(2) In the second place, proleptic ethics is dualistic in the sense that the new reality of the future kingdom is already operative under the conditions of this present age—this sinful world. The future of the kingdom—though still future—makes a decisive difference in the present; that is, it releases power for new decisions that may run counter to the established trends and current norms. The ethical question is what to do "meanwhile," between the time of the initial penetration of the new and the time when all resistance to it shall fade away. If the new is genuinely overlapping the old, there is an ambiguity in every act, resulting from the simultaneity of the Christian's participation in what the New Testament calls the two aeons. Luther's description of the existential situation of the Christian as *simul iustus et peccator* must be reinterpreted within the horizon of proleptic eschatology.

(3) In the third place, the ethics of eschatological love translates itself into an ethics of power and justice under the conditions of a sinful world that has not yet been apocalyptically transformed into the new world of God's future. The roots of

love and justice are not ultimately heterogeneous; rather, the principle of justice is built into love that seeks the fulfillment of the other person. The element of justice is implicit in the principle, "love your neighbor *as yourself*," for the core of justice is care for the other person. Now, the accomplishment of justice can be motivated either by the presence of love or the pressure of law. Justice is too important a matter to leave to loving persons. There are not enough of them around. Therefore, normally we think of justice in terms of law with power to back it up. Justice is to be done, the other person is to be cared for, whether anyone is moved by love or not. Luther's picture of the two arms of God is acceptable, the arm of justice according to law and the arm of mercy according to gospel, provided we also stress the one heart of love that moves them both.

(4) In the fourth place, love that expresses itself through justice and law is not at all antithetical to principles and rules that can be clearly formulated to prescribe as well as to guide the ethical decisions and moral actions of human beings. The antinomian idea that love is unmediated by principle is a case of too big a dose of docetism. First gnosticism gave rise to the docetic notion that the Word of God could not become the body of man, then it escaped into dogmatics decreeing that the truth of God and his gospel could not be uttered in propositional terms, in reasonable assertions, and now it has made its appearance in situation ethics forbidding the translation of love and justice into moral principles that can be normatively applied in concrete ethical situations.

(5) In the fifth place, just as eschatological ethics sits loose to a strict identification of itself with either deontology or teleology, so also it refuses to ally itself exclusively with one of Frankena's sub-types of classification, namely, rule-agapism, act-agapism, or summary rule-agapism. When love expresses itself through the structures of justice, there are rules that can be formulated in advance of each new situation, for example, with respect to liberty and equality, which we all take for granted, as though they were intuitions that erupted spontaneously from each of us. The notion that there are no rules, but only situations, is an unrealistic appraisal of the human condition outside of paradise. Even in Eden there was one rule to remind man and woman of their moral adolescence and their distance from a state of fulfillment in which there will be only love and no rules anymore.

Act-agapism carries an element of truth in that creative love opens a person to new opportunities and new responsibilities that have not yet been grasped by the common sense of justice and enacted into law. Thus, love can be expressed through law, but it can also extend beyond it in response to unique elements in a contingent situation, expressing the freedom and novelty of love. Summary rule-agapism captures the notion that the ways and works of love, that first broke through where there were no rules, may now be summarized *ex post facto* as useful aids for others in quest of guidelines for their expressions of love. Thus, an ethics of love relates to law in a dialectically differentiated way, true to the complexities of the human situation so conditioned by the continuities of the old and the novelties of the eschatologically new.

(6) In the sixth place, eschatological ethics not only translates the dynamics of love into forms of justice operative in this given world, but also injects norms of the future into the contexts of the present. The former illuminates the orientation of law in the Old Testament, the latter the definition of law in the New Testament. There is a fundamental difference, because the appearance of the apocalyptic future in Jesus puts an end to the law by announcing its fulfillment. Hence, Jesus is not a second Moses; the Sermon on the Mount presupposes eschatological provisions of the kingdom, whereas the Tables of the Law presuppose the historical covenants of Jahweh with his people. Therefore, while the rule of justice through law continues, a new law of love is at work in the same contexts of life. This means that eschatological ethics is as contextual as any; however, contextual ethics does not mean in this case "getting the facts straight" and then "doing what comes naturally." It does not mean letting the context determine the action; its contextualism may express itself counter-culturally. Contextual ethics that popularly goes by the name is often an excuse merely to go down stream, to go with the contextual trends. Eschatological ethics widens the context, so that the future that is not yet a part of a given context may reveal the norms to change it and create a new and better context. There are two kinds of contextual ethics, one that gives in to the present context, another that calls for it to change in conformity with transcendent norms that emanate from the eschatological future.

(7) In the seventh place, eschatological ethics has universal

validity, and is not confined to the context of the Christian
koinonia. The eschatological future of the kingdom is the power
that draws all men, whether they know it or not. This power
has been revealed in the Christ-event as the highest good which
all men seek in the quest of personal identity-in-fulfillment. A
philosophical analysis of the structure of human action discloses
a striving for an envisioned good that is absent in the present.
Ethical action is therefore constituted by the negation of evil
here and now and an affirmation of a transcendent good that is
future and yet to be fulfilled. This highest good which Jesus
identified as the kingdom of God in his message can be seen
retrospectively to be the power at work in every human quest
for fulfillment. Therefore, the kingdom of God is proleptically
present in all moral systems of mankind as the power of their
end, and not only inside the ghetto of a Christian *koinonia*.
This presence of the kingdom of God in the universal human
striving for the good has been called the "natural law" in the
classical tradition. The theory of "natural law" has fortunately
been kept alive in the moral theology of Roman Catholicism,
but regrettably in a thoroughly non-eschatological form. The
values of this tradition can be taken up into the framework of
eschatological ethics.

(8) In the eighth place, the ethics of the kingdom of God provide a single point of departure for personal, social and ecological ethics. The dichotomy between personal and political ethics
is overcome by the idea of the kingdom of God as the starting
point for Christian ethics. There are not two strictly heterogeneous ethics, one for the realm of personal relations, another
in the secular realm of social relations, political institutions,
and the care of the earth. The non-eschatological form of the
two-kingdom ethic in traditional Lutheranism has triggered
revolutionary explosions in the depth dimensions of personal
experience, but has invariably reinforced conservative impulses
in the realm of government and law. The link between eschatology and political ethics is as legitimate as its link to personal
ethics. Paul Tillich has shown that the biblical symbol of the
kingdom of God has political, social, personalistic and universal
characteristics.[22] It is the task of eschatological ethics to draw
out fully the implications of these facets of the kingdom of God.

(9) In the ninth place, the twin accent on love and fulfillment in eschatological ethics puts it at war with every authori-

tarian form of obedience. Obedience to *nomos* is a virtue that favors those who hold power and authority; it keeps their subjects submissive and perpetuates the status quo. The stress on the eschatological future elevates the power of imagination and transcendent vision, to make way for the advent of new possibilities that are only now appearing on the horizon. Bultmann has coined the term "radical obedience," but I believe with Dorothee Sölle [23] that too many crimes have been committed in the name of obedience to the state to make it useful in describing the believer's openness to the oncoming future of God's kingdom. Christians like others must render obedience to law and those in authority, but their relation to the kingdom of God is not another instance of such obedience. That would merit its being called heteronomous ethics. Tillich's discussion of the relations between theonomous, autonomous, and heteronomous ethics can be appropriated also by eschatological ethics.

(10) In the tenth place, in proleptic ethics it may truly be said that the end justifies the means, because the end is proleptically present and operative beforehand, rehearsing the qualities of the eschatological kingdom—peace, love, joy, freedom, equality, unity—in the course of history's forward movement. The use of evil means for allegedly good ends, often charged to messianic movements in history, including Marxism, is morally unacceptable, no matter what the ends. For the end that justifies is a future good that makes a present impact by bringing the means under judgment.

(11) In the eleventh place, the idea of the proleptic presence of the eschatological future provides a bridge to the truth in dispositional ethics. Being precedes act; a new state of being is the source of a new stream of acts. However, this new state of being is itself the act of God—a miracle of sheer grace—and not something that can be willed into being. The Kantian ethic of duty fails because it assumes that the moral imperative will naturally encounter or have the power to generate a willing response. But there is no health that comes from the law. Grace alone provides the new ground of being in man, making the unwilling will for the first time willing to do what love commands. The ethical *Aufgabe* is radically dependent on the religious *Gabe*.

(12) In the twelfth place, the life-style commended by a future-oriented ethic may be conceived of as *eschatopraxis*—doing the

future now ahead of time. Believers have made the greatest impact for the good in history when they have been somewhat out
of joint with the times. They have acted on the impulses of a
vision, on intuitions that run ahead to meet an approaching
future. The power of this future does not seduce those who love
it to leave the world; rather, it invites them to direct their love
of God back into the world, to care for the earth and all his living creatures. The coming of the eschatological future is down-
to-earth, and exempts those who expect it from having to flee
elsewhere to meet it.

To conclude this chapter, we offer a starkly simple recapitulation: the *leitmotiv* is the future eschatological kingdom of
God that has become proleptically present in a definitive way in
Jesus of Nazareth. This determines the *goal* of ethics—the kingdom of God as the highest good. The materially definitive content of the eschatological rule that is revealed in the ministry of
Jesus is love. This determines the *norm* of ethics—the *agape* of
God as the absolute norm underlying all principles of justice
and equality, etc. The proleptic presence of the kingdom of
God makes possible a real participation in the new reality that
it brings. This determines the *motive* of ethics—the motivating
force of the new being in Christ.

Finally, there is the *context* of the ethical decision. Goals,
norms, and motives converge upon a concrete context, not to
invite us to groove in, but to challenge and to change the present
conditions in the direction of a better approximation of the
kingdom of God.

8

The One-sided
Politics of
the Kingdom

One-Sided Politics

It is becoming difficult to do theology today without getting involved in politics. The reason is that every element in our lives has become political. Once a person takes a stand on a political issue, he has taken sides. Being one-sided can be an unpleasant experience. It is particularly unpleasant for a Christian, because he is placed in a tension between two roles—being an agent of reconciliation and an agent of polarization. The pastor of a congregation realizes this sooner than any other Christian. If he gets mixed up in politics, he inescapably finds himself in a potentially polarizing situation. People will rally around him enthusiastically, in the urge to secure some divine sanction for their cause; or they will plant themselves squarely against him and write off their pastor as an agent of the enemy. Very soon there is a perceptible effect on church attendance and the Sunday offerings. One or two costly sorties into political activity can drive the pastor back into the safer sanctuary of pious rhetoric. One has to ponder whether or not to back-track to a message of private salvation, and leave politics to others.

Politics, however, is impossible to escape. If religion once imagined that it could stick to existential problems, it can do so no more, for political and existential issues converge. When theology avoids the task of interpreting the political realities of the day, it runs the risk of becoming an ideology of the established order. We are learning that there is no political bomb-proof shelter for theology; there is no demilitarized zone, where theology can contemplate lofty eternal values, or remain perched on stilts of ecclesiastical neutrality. Theologians, church leaders and pastors—the clergy in general—have been accustomed to thinking of themselves as a little bit above and beyond the necessity of taking sides. Should not agents of reconciliation be beyond politics and therefore beyond polarization? This may be a comforting rationalization to serve the self-interest of the empirical church and its leadership, but it certainly does not come from the message the church is called to preach and live. Sometimes polarization is the inevitable result of the Christian's witness to the gospel. Panting for premature reconciliation may be a weak spasm of pseudo-love that plays into the hands of those on the top. If the slave and the master have a falling out, it is a dirty trick to get them subjectively reconciled before the slave gains an objectively new arrangement that spells freedom for him.

The fate of genuine love in the polarizing situations of worldly politics has been placarded for all eyes to see in the crucifixion of Jesus of Nazareth. The Christian can hardly demand a kindlier fate than his Master. No one gets crucified unless he has been trapped in a polarizing situation. Jesus was unable to keep peace in Israel while bringing in the righteousness of the kingdom. As long as he was silent, there was no trouble. But when he began to state his meaning, the call went out for his arrest. He was grabbed by the police, jeered by the crowd, and brought to trial for the truth that he spoke. Jesus entered into solidarity with the left out and the cast out; for this one-sided action he became marked for suffering. He was murdered by the system of law and order which he seemed to threaten. He was not the pitiful victim of tragic misunderstanding, mistaken identity or a communication gap. A sensitivity marathon would not have changed the outcome. He really was a threat to the system; his truth really did create a polarizing situation; his therapy was more than the existing order could accommodate. For Jesus to have ascended into a cloud of sweet talk about love and harmony, stepping aside from the encounter with the officers of the system, would have meant the betrayal of the kingdom he represented. He could not mix the truth of God with the lies of the world. This unrelenting consistency for the kingdom's sake was spelled out in the world in the shape of a cross.

Perhaps the one-sided politics of the kingdom always takes the shape of the cross in world history. The road to the kingdom is still lined by bodies racked up on crosses. Of course, no Christian longs for the cross. But he must be watchful lest the message of love is perverted into a calculus to avoid the cross. In our century we have had a chain of crosses on which Jews and Blacks and Indians and Chicanos and Vietnamese have been slaughtered. On the day of judgment nice decent people in the churches will be handed their share of the bill for the crimes of history committed before their eyes. The peace of the church must be disturbed as long as "the little ones" in history are being offended. The Spirit has created the people of Jesus to be the advocate of the poor and the oppressed. When they join the politics of the silent majority, they enter into self-contradiction, the visible antithesis of their true being.

This one-sided aspect of Christian existence in the world is often disguised from us because we are accustomed to viewing our own Protestant heroes as basically church reformers. Luther, for example, is pictured by his followers as a preacher who rediscovered the gospel and started a movement to reform the church. They see it exclusively as an intramural affair of concern only to Christians. This is to forget that when Luther said, "Here I stand," he was on trial in a political courtroom—the Diet of Worms in 1521. This picture is in stark contrast to the Luther standing at a chapel door tacking up his 95 theses—all religious propositions. But at Worms Luther was on trial as a political criminal for preaching a message that meant more freedom than the empire cared to grant at that point in time. Luther knew what it meant to be a fugitive from the law. The law had become lawless and an instrument of oppression. The image of Luther at Worms reminds us that a spiritual revolution of the gospel will always have repercussions in Caesar's realm. Both the emperor and the papacy conspired against Luther's call for freedom. This made Luther both a heretic of the church and an outlaw in the empire.

The accusation against Luther was not that he was too radical as a reformer. Rather, he was charged and chased as a revolutionary. He was accused of inciting the German people to riot. He was quoted as saying that "the Germans should wash their hands in the blood of the papists." In the edict of Worms it was charged that Luther's teachings were fostering rebellion, polarization, war, murder, robbery, arson, attacking the foundations on which the great society was built. This image of Luther as a freedom fighter standing trial in a political tribunal is one aspect his heirs should bear in mind, in view of their counter-revolutionary history. Those who bear his name have forgotten his revolution for freedom; instead they have portrayed him as a conservative reformer, even as a biblical fundamentalist.

Religion as Protest

Polarizing politics came to America during its imperialist attack on the people of Viet Nam and Cambodia. Never have Americans been so divided since the Civil War. Bumper stickers were saying: "Love it or leave it." Some left it to escape the draft and in protest against the war. Many fathers saw their sons as though they were committing the unforgivable sin. Ironically, many of the fathers of these fathers came to America with the waves of immigrants who left the old country for the same reason our young people have left—to be free not to kill other human beings. Strange that Christians should have to be reminded that one of God's commandments is against killing! Nowhere is it written that the prohibition against killing can be lifted when the leaders of the nation decide to conscript young people to kill in the interest of their country's evil desires. In recent years we have heard too many Christians mouthing the idolatrous slogan: my country right or wrong.

The killing is now over. But America is still at war. It is at war with itself. The issue of amnesty is the concrete expression of this inner struggle. To us amnesty is the least that we can offer in exchange for the righteous protest of young people against the immorality of their leaders. Christians should keep the issue of amnesty within the perspective of their own history of faith. They should remember the story of Abraham, the father of all the faithful. Abraham left his country when he heard the command: "Go from your country and your fellow countrymen, and leave your father's house." In today's idiom this means that there is a higher call than the draft board's to serve one's country. There is a higher call than loyalty to the nation and to its leaders who prosecute its wars. The American dream has turned into a nightmare by this Archie Bunker style of patriotism. The values of the American dream—life, liberty and the pursuit of happiness—are worthy of great sacrifice. When John F. Kennedy cried, "Ask not what your country can do for you, but ask what you can do for your country," he had in mind the essential values on which that nation was founded, and not the corrupt political hacks who served as fronts for the military-industrial complex.

Christianity is drawn into the struggle to identify the goals and values worthy of loyalty and sincere commitment in political terms. The polarization in America has revealed a split soul within the churches. The one side puts the faith at the disposal of patriotism, the other makes it the motive power of dissent. In the sixties it seemed that the pendulum of religion had swung to the side of protest. We thought we were done with religion as the sweet honey of positive thinking on the comb of middle-class society. Religion erupted with a righteous noise on the side of the oppressed minorities, undertaking the advocacy of radical causes, joining the parade of the liberation movements at home and abroad. The clerical collar could be seen in the streets—in the struggle for civil rights, in peace demonstrations, and siding with the youth in its attack on the establishment. The clergyman got the image of being some kind of radical, more interested in the plight of the migrant workers than in the parochial needs back home. He was called, he felt, to deal with the big problems out there, so he neglected the little people in the shadows of his own parish. He had a romance going with inner city people, the poor and the blacks, and spoke contemptuously of the well-groomed people who came regularly to church and paid his salary.

In the seventies we are witnessing a backlash. Parish leaders have begun a protest of their own against a religion of protest. They pay the bills; they are going to call the tune. The pendulum has swung the other way. Back to the boonies! Experimental ministries have been called off; monies for mission are drying up; ordained women can't get jobs. There is a desire to return to the flesh pots of a spiritual religion—the religious boom of the fifties. This was at least part of the motive behind Key 73.

The Ethnic Factor

One unmistakable symptom of the religious backlash is the new stress on ethnocentric identity. The man with the picket had his turn; now it's time for the man with the lunch pail. Charles Reich in *Greening of America* captured the mood of the the late sixties; Peter Berger has spoken of the new mood as "the blueing of America." And Michael Novak has put it all together in his book, *The Rise of the Unmeltable Ethnics.* There are religious implications of this ethnocentric trend. It will reinforce the tie of religion to the past, not to the specifically Christian resources in the past, but to the religious culture of our ethnic origins. The danger is that Christianity will fall back into the frame of ethnic religion, and lose its future orientation and universal perspective.

Yet, the new ethnic consciousness may have its element of truth—its necessary service to render. It can free all Americans from the destructive myth of the melting pot. A Jewish immigrant, Israel Zangwill, cried ecstatically in 1908: "America is God's crucible, the great Melting Pot where all races are merging." The melting pot was a refuge for many people, but it became an oppression for others. In the archives of the Ford Motor Company there is a text that tells about a graduation ceremony of the Ford English school. It reads: "Commencement exercises were held in the largest hall in the city. On the stage was represented an immigrant ship. In front of it was a huge melting pot. Down the gang plank came the members of the class dressed in their national garbs and carrying luggage such as they carried when they landed in this country. Down they poured into the Ford melting pot and disappeared. Then the teachers began to stir the contents of the pot with long ladles. Presently the pot began to boil over and out came the men dressed in their best American clothes and waving American flags." [1]

The new ethnicity has broken the spell of the melting pot myth. Becoming assimilated into the American process as we know it is no longer home to the land of freedom. In his *Letters From an American Farmer*, 1782, Michel de Crevecoeur called the American the "new Adam." That is no longer credible to us. We could just as well call him the "old Roman." Here in America, Crevecoeur said, individuals from all nations are being melted into a new race of beautiful men. It was a great dream; now "American" stands for a plastic culture, artificial food, and a lot of dirty habits—at least for many people here and abroad. The return to ethnicity may be a useful retreat from this ugly melting pot in which a rich pluralism of differences becomes assimilated into a one-dimensional culture. It may help break the back of a repressive bureaucracy in control of a mindless, soul-

less and rootless mass society and restore pride in a variety of
alternatives that were being lost in the melting pot.

We cannot, however, adopt the new ethnicity as a promising
model for Christianity. In a struggle between the ethnic factor
and the melting pot, we could even go to the defense of ethnicity. One person's *eth* is as good as another's. But Christianity
is a universal religion; it does not fall into any ethnic bag whatsoever. This is the Abrahamic drive in Christianity. To say that
Abraham is the father of us all is to hear the call of God to go
beyond ethnicity. Abraham started with ethnicity, happy at
hearth and home, rooted in blood and soil. Then he heard the
command of God: "Go from your homeland!" Leave your father's house and all the local gods and their favorite dishes. Go
from your homeland of ethnic origins to a new "homeland of
identity" which is still a thing of the future for us all. The
essential identity of a Christian is not determined by where he
comes from, scribbled on his birth certificate. It is given by the
goal to which he is moving, declared at his new birth in baptism
and written on the heart by the Spirit. This new identity is
grounded in the essential future of all men in the kingdom of
God. In the fullness of God's kingdom there is a unity in being
that transcends all racial, ethnic, linguistic, national and religious boundaries. This gospel is the hope of a badly split humanity. Christians should be proud of their ethnicity, but only
as their starting point in the realm of creation. Ethnicity is the
given of each man's concrete history. But there is something
better in the future.

Two Types of Theology

Whether the issue is polarization, protest, amnesty, or ethnicity, we are dealing with ethical problems the solution of which
must lead back to basic theological decisions. There is a civil
war going on in Christianity that can be traced back to the earliest origins of religion in the Bible. Just as the English states-
man Disraeli complained that the English people were splitting
into "two nations," because of the widening breach between the
new class of rich people and the great mass of paupers, similarly we are suffering today from the splitting of Christianity
into two factions. Or perhaps it is the classical struggle between

Jacob and Esau going on within the heart of each believer, now being pulled to one side, now to the other.

Throughout the history of Christianity there has been a relentless battle between two faiths, two types of theology, two styles of relating to the world around. The one we could call the traditional-institutional type, the other the apocalyptic-revolutionary type. The traditional type sees religion as order. It functions as the priest bestowing divine legitimacy on the established order. It came into its own under Emperor Constantine. This traditional-institutional type would not agree to the charge that it is heartlessly disinterested in the plight of the poor and the oppressed. On the contrary, it has always boasted of holding out to them a hope for the biggest prize of all—heaven above in a life after death. What do a few years of poverty and misery matter in the long run? If one perseveres in patience in tribulation, nothing less than eternal life is the reward. Heaven is an available system of relief from the pains of earth.

Against this there stands the apocalyptic trend that puts heaven to work as the criticism of earth. There is a heavenly critique of earthly existence. It does not teach mere resignation in face of exploitation, but liberation from oppression. It tries to take seriously the simplest prayer to God that his "will be done *on earth* as it is in heaven." Apocalyptic religion is far from being an opium to the masses; it is the leaven of heaven in the earthly bread that is rising to new dimensions of freedom. If the institutional approach has often co-existed with class dominations and repressive regimes, the apocalyptic trend has led the movement of protest in the revolutionary struggle against the established order.

Two Symbols: Space and Time

The civil war in religion, between religion as patriotism and religion as protest, can be depicted in the categories of space and time. This war was going on between Israel and her pagan neighbors. Paganism puts its gods in definite spaces. It is natural for people to want their own space, their own earth and soil, as they have their own body and soul. However, when the power of God is connected with these special places, then the unity of God's power and being is fragmented and pluralized, and the result is polytheism. Many spaces with absolute meaning give rise to many gods. In Israel's faith this means that any soil or section of the earth that makes arrogant and unlimited claims for itself becomes demonic. The god of one land and people struggles against the gods of all surrounding countries.

We are not dealing only with an ancient phenomenon of religion. For there is a neo-paganism alive today wherever people are kept in spatial bondage to the gods of race or color, of nation or ethnic origin. These are powerful gods which bestow absolute status on a particular racial community or a special nationality. When a nation can cause a person to make the ultimate sacrifice of his life to its national crusade, right or wrong, it is acting as the god of that space who holds the ultimate decision of life or death in its pockets. For this reason every nation tries to make its war into a holy crusade, to justify a total, unconditional loyalty on the part of its citizens.

But there is another God who reaches into history as the God of time, who makes himself known in the struggle to liberate those kept in spatial bondage to the gods of this world. The command of this God to Abraham to break with the past can be heard to echo in the words of Jesus: "If anyone comes to me and does not hate his own father and mother and wife and children and brothers and sisters, yes, and even his own life, he cannot be my disciple" (Luke 14:26). The God who spoke to and through Abraham and Jesus cannot be identified with a family or nation, not even with the interests of Christianity or our church. This God raises up prophets to create a religion of protest against the priests of soil and blood; the great prophets were willing to carry the message of this God against the nation of Israel itself and pronounce judgment upon it. In fact, New Testament Christianity could call itself the "true Israel" because it brought about the de-nationalization of the religion of Israel.

Abraham is still for us the symbol of freedom from spatial bondage; he is the symbol of the man of faith who responds to the call, not from the god-at-home, but from the alien Word. This Word of God is alien because he is a stranger to the local gods of the givens of hearth and home, nation, race and ethnic identity. This new God of history means to bless *all* the nations and races of the earth. This is why this God of the Jews and of Jesus is a threat to every religious nationalism.

The biblical believer is always being converted by the God of history from the closedness of monadic existence into the open-ness of a nomadic style of life. He becomes like an alien, living beyond the borders of his own country, on his way to a home-land that turns strangers into friends. He is going forth from the homeland of his birth to a new homeland which the Lord will show him. At times this can mean to break with the ruling authorities, to confound the prevailing social and political pat-terns, and to join in resistance when necessary. It can mean de-parting from traditional beliefs and institutional rules; it can mean entering into a process of radical inquiry, opening up new paths to the mystery of the unknown. In the words of Friedrich Nietzsche, it means moving into "the land of our children" and out of "the land of our fathers and mothers." This is an exodus in time, moving from spatial bondage into temporal freedom in history. This new homeland, the alien country into which we are called, is not another space, not a space among others that we can isolate and defend like an armed camp. It is the realm of the future luring us beyond the frontiers of the present. The God of the universal future of mankind joins all individual spaces into one planetary world, bestowing an international consciousness on a diaspora-people moving forward in history, making them aliens in any single country, but citizens of them all.

The experience of Israel and of the church in history proves how difficult it is to be loyal to the God of time. The tempta-tion is severe to fall back upon the gods of space and to wrap oneself in the comforts they promise. In this light one can raise serious questions about the revival of the spatial element in the Zionist movement. Rabbi Richard Rubenstein intentionally shocks his readers when he says that after Auschwitz Jews can no longer believe in the God of history. He says that since "the God of history is dead, we will have to return to a religion of nature. We will come to know once again the primitive earth-deities, Baal and Astarte, whom Israel forsook to become Jah-weh's chosen people with a mission in history." [2] Rubenstein calls for a clean-cut decision between the God of time and the God of space, the God of history and the God of nature. The gods of space and nature are stationary symbols of comfort. The God of history is the author of an exodus community with a mission to all nations, to announce the coming rule of a uni-versal freedom, justice, happiness and shalom for all.

Rabbi Rubenstein has ignored the fact that in forsaking the

God of history, he is turning away from the God of Abraham and turning instead to the earth deities of *"Blut und Boden"* of Nazi Germany which paved the way for Hitler to create an Auschwitz in the first place. Hitler's god was the natural religion of space. With a deadly consistency he attacked the Jews who bore the memories and the rituals of the God of history. The racial myths of the twentieth century, directed first against the Jews and then against the Blacks, have absolutely no support in the historical myth of Jahweh and his covenant people. These are the neo-pagan myths that hail from the gods of space and soil, of racial blood and closed borders. Gods with color in their cheeks are no gods at all.

It has been very difficult to locate our essential freedom and loyalty in a non-spatial future. Israel herself looked toward the day when all nations would come to Mount Zion in Palestine. Western Christianity bound its soul to the sacred space in Rome, until the Reformation became a protesting movement negating this spatial bondage, once again picking up the biblical beat of a people on the move, forming protesting pockets of resistance in all the lands. But even the Protestant groups could not live long without their new sacred spaces. The Calvinists had their Geneva and their Puritan descendants founded their theocracies in America. At first the God of history drew people together out of all nations in pursuit of the millenium. It was to be the kingdom of God in microcosm, the melting pot of all the nations, a beacon of hope that the demonic system of nation-states in Europe, leading to war after war, could be overcome. America was to spawn a new future of universal hope to all the nations, bearing a vision that could serve and foster the development of all the peoples of the world. Every man and woman in America carried in their hearts a few impulses of millenial enthusiasm for the future, so that even when its soldiers went forth to war, it was never merely to satisfy an imperialistic drive like the other nations presumably had, but only to make the world safe for democracy, to build a better tomorrow and make a lasting peace.

But now a great uncertainty has supervened. The "righteous empire" (Martin Marty) is beginning to have serious doubts about itself. It looks and acts like the other empire-beasts that have come and gone. Its mission in the world is no longer moved by ideals and higher values. Watergate reveals that a frightening portion of its soul has gone over to the gods of space, belligerently erecting fences, walls and curtains, forsaking the dream of one world that can become Everyman's garden, and going to great lengths to threaten to convert the earth into a barren smoking ruin, turning its ploughshares back into the swords our fathers wanted to leave behind in a militaristic Europe.

National Socialism and Religious Socialism

The god of space is nationalistic. Under its sovereignty, man the national patriot clashes with man the world citizen. In Hitler's Germany national socialism was able to gain support from some churchmen and theologians. There was the memorable conflict between the great Lutheran church historian Emmanuel Hirsch, and the Lutheran systematic theologian, Paul Tillich. This was a clash between a theology of national socialism and a theology of religious socialism.[3] The ideology of national socialism was not born first with Hitler; and the end of World War II did not put an end to it. It is a recurring possibility that comes by the sanctification of nationalism. In Germany it can be traced back to Johann Fichte. What a tragic person! In his youth he was a fanatic champion of the French revolution, almost an anarchist advocating extreme views on liberty, equality and fraternity. But in the year 1800 he made a complete about-face, making a vigorous plea for law and order, national discipline and solidarity. He projects for the German people a utopian state, a closed commercial state, a radical state socialism which is basically absolutistic and despotic. Individual liberties have to be curbed by repressive measures for the sake of the general welfare. In almost Skinnerian fashion he proposes a completely centralized planned economy, with a precise calculus of production, distribution and consumption under state authority. In this closed economy he sees a permanent balance between the *needs* of the people and the *means* of the people, and this, of course, is only possible if the geographical assets of the country permit it. If this is not yet the case, then the country has every right to widen is natural boundaries to gain the necessary *Lebensraum*. This is exactly the course that Hitler followed. He was only reaching the goal of the proper natural boundaries of the sealed-off state. In Fichte's utopia the true German people no longer seek or need contact with the outside world. Their mission is to cultivate a national consciousness, to develop the unique national folk-character, to stimulate a patriotic zeal for an *"echt-deutsch"*—a true German—nation. The goal of the god is to create a folk and a fatherland of the purest racial strain and the noblest culture.

Emmanuel Hirsch, together with many other Germans, believed that Hitler was the right man at the right time to make Fichte's utopia a reality. His theological basis for this was the famous—or the infamous—doctrine of the natural orders of creation. Even after World War II Werner Elert, an Erlangen theologian, could teach that *Das Volk,* a radically homogeneous people, is one of the natural orders, with clear boundaries that God has made. Each person is assigned by God to a specific national group based on blood affinity, and must exercise his moral functions within its limitations. Here we have the naturalistic god of space giving its signature to modern nationalism. Patriotism is then the highest duty of the citizen, the basic law of nature, underwritten by the God of creation. The pious believer would hardly think to challenge the ruling authorities. The theology of his church teaches submission to the higher authorities. The duty of the citizen is to be obedient, to follow the rule.

Against this line of thinking there was the religious socialist position of Paul Tillich and his friends. Most of them were soon forced into exile. They proved to be poor religious nationalists. As part of the new proletarian consciousness, religious socialism projected a unity of mankind that swept over the whole world, uniting people of all countries, as a religious anticipation of the truth in the idea of the kingdom of God to which all nations and all races belong with equal dignity and honor. The rifts and rivalries between my native country and an alien land are transcended in my consciousness, because I am first of all a member of the human race, only secondarily a member of the white race. I am first of all a citizen of this planet earth, only secondarily a citizen of the United States. Voltaire, the very opposite of Fichte, was blamed for being a man first, and only thereafter a Frenchman. He was accused of pouring cold water into the hot springs of the folk-love *de la Patrie*—of the fatherland.

Religious socialism was trying to be the politics of the kingdom of God in a planetary age. It was a collosal failure in the Germany of the thirties, but I believe it was mainly in the right. It does not deny the limited truth of nationalism. There is a place for group loyalty, national patriotism, ethnic pride and love of one's own people. We could even say that just as a person cannot love others if he does not love himself, so he cannot be a good religious socialist, a citizen of world history, without taking seriously the geography of his own individual existence. We all start with certain *givens* in our life. You are the child of a particular couple, with one father and one mother, with a particular set of experiences in history that no one else has ever had, sharing in a particular culture, and speaking a particular language. You have a right to be proud of all that. Your folkways and customs, your manner of dress and domesticity, your eating and sleeping habits, your ethnic games and folk music, are all as good as any others, simply because they are yours.

Abraham did not leave his native homeland because he was a misfit. A person does not become a world missionary necessarily because he is unhappy at home. He also loves his native land. He feels as truly patriotic as anyone else. But he has been captured by a transcendent vision of promise for all his earthly brothers. He lives beyond his native identity toward an alien identity that constitutes his essential future, placing him in solidarity with all those who, though they are not part of his native beginning, may nevertheless be integral to his ultimate fulfillment. So his vision has universal scope! His essential future is not determined by an accident of birth. Man is not an animal, despite all resemblances. He can be open to the future and live beyond his given environment. He is not limited by the accidents of his birth, by the features of his national, cultural, and racial origin. Transcendence and futurity and universality are part of his essential destiny as man. These features are gifts of the God of history.

What can we expect in the near future? Which of the two tracks we have sketched will win out—religion as spatially centered, supporting nationalistic patriotism, ethnic pride or tribal loyalty, or religion as a liberation movement, overcoming the dichotomies which paint a future of black against white, of rich nations against poor nations, of children against parents, of the East against the West? Under the conditions of existence there is no way to make a perfectly unambiguous decision for one side or the other. We love the old watering holes; we like to return to the old shrines. There is too much nature romanticism in us to be able to endure the hardy wilderness life of the pilgrims on their way to the future kingdom. We all hanker to return to our favorite flesh pots. Perhaps we find ourselves at best torn by a double loyalty, suffering a tension of soul between God and mammon, between the self-interests of our native land and the interests of the world's people, so that while we are enjoying the banquet of the rich man, Lazarus is having his sores licked by dogs. We cannot attain the pure conscience of the zealot nor maintain the rigorous consistency of the martyr. We are schizo-phrenics of the kingdom of God, split within ourselves, volunteering for a mission to tear down fences and curtains behind which we still like to hide, enjoying protections, privileges and immunities that these deny to others.

The conflict between the two types of religion will increase. There will still be oppression, tribulation and persecution for those who choose the narrow way. Jesus said, "They will put you out of the synagogues; indeed, the hour is coming when whoever kills you will think he is offering service to God" (John 16:2).

9

Theory and Praxis:
Reflections on
an Old Theme

Introduction

Immanuel Kant once wrote a treatise challenging the popular saying, "This may be correct as far as theory goes but is worthless in practice." [1] He argued that the value of a particular ethical practice depends entirely on its correspondence with ethical theory. To claim that ethics holds true in theory but not in practice is as ridiculous, Kant says, as if an engineer would argue that even though its theoretical laws are well worked out, ballistics does not apply in practice, "since in practice experience yields results quite different from those of theory." [2] Countless times I have had occasion to object to a deplorable divorce between theory and practice in theological education. What we believe, teach, and confess in dogmatic categories may be held as true in theory, but simply ignored as too impractical to carry through in our parish programs. We may teach like Augustinians, but act like Pelagians; we may confess the Nicene Creed, but preach like Arians. In this presentation I would like to offer a critique of theological education on the basis of certain reflections on the relation between theory and praxis. I would implicitly defend the Kantian proposition that "if something holds true in theory on rational grounds, it holds true for practice as well." [3]

I am urged to find a mutually reinforcing relation between theory and praxis, because I am as opposed to the hostility to theoretical concepts that we first met in student activism and that now flourishes in the sensitivity movement as I am to the older dogmaticism that built a "house of cards" out of true biblical doctrines that had no connection with the lived experiences of believers and no practical links to empirical verification pro-

138

cedures. To use a Kantian type of expression, theory without praxis is empty, while praxis without theory is blind.

The Turn to Praxis

In the history of theology there are times when a particular concept captures the imagination of a whole group or generation of thinkers. Think of such terms as kerygma, demythologizing, *Heilsgeschichte,* Word of God, secular Christianity, theology of hope, etc. Today the concept of praxis is taking its turn at catching the magic that turns on a whole generation. Of course, the concept was not first born yesterday, but it is being born again in present-day liberation theology. Gustavo Gutierrez, Latin American author of *A Theology of Liberation,* integrates the concept of praxis into his definition of theology. He states that theology is critical reflection on the historical praxis of the church involved in the liberating process through which the world is transformed.[4]

The pre-history of the concept of praxis in modern times goes back to the attempt of the Left Wing Hegelians to go beyond Hegel who had transfigured the traditional symbols of faith into speculative philosophical concepts. In going beyond Hegel they called for reconciliation, not in the sphere of abstract thinking but within the material conditions of concrete history. The first one among these Left Wing Hegelians to use the concept of praxis as fundamental to philosophy was A. V. Cieszkowski. He said that the task of philosophy was "to become a practical philosophy or rather a philosophy of practical activity, of 'praxis', exercising a direct influence on social life and developing the future in the realm of concrete activity." [5] Bruno Bauer went even further. In 1841 he wrote: "Philosophy wants a revolution, a revolution against everything positive, including history." [6] The philosopher's brain was to become a trigger for a *Sturz des Bestehenden,* for an overthrow of the existing order. Karl Marx went even further, elaborating this theory of revolutionary praxis as the criticism of all theory, as revealing the backward character of all philosophizing to that point in time. Not theory but praxis becomes the new lever of salvation.

Marx's "Theses on Feuerbach" have become the "Bible" for the current reception of Marxist praxiology into theological language. How many times have we not read in favorable light

Marx's eleventh thesis: "The philosophers have only interpreted the world in various ways; the point is, to *change* it." That reads like holy writ in contemporary theology. It has acquired axiomatic status among theologians of hope. But all of Marx's theses run in the same vein. The first thesis stresses the significance of revolutionary or practical-critical activity. The second asserts that the question whether human thinking can reach objective truth is not a theoretical but a practical question. The third says that the circumstances of life can be changed only through revolutionary practice. And the other theses follow up these ideas. Praxis becomes the key to understanding Marx's philosophy.

This Marxist notion of praxis has made a great impact on theologians who have been involved in the theology of hope (Jürgen Moltmann), political theology (J. B. Metz) or theology of liberation (Gustavo Gutierrez). Consider Moltmann's statement: "The new criterion of theology and of faith is to be found in praxis." [7] He means that praxis has become the test of a theory. Truth must be practical; it must contain the initiative for changing the world for the better, that is, as a better approximation of the kingdom of God. Christian hope becomes practical in the transformation of the present. Then listen to J. B. Metz: "A new relation between theory and practice, between knowledge and morality, between reflection and revolution, will have to be worked out, and it will have to determine theological thought, if theological thought is not to be left at a pre-critical stage. Henceforth, practical and, in the widest sense of the word, political reason must take part in all critical reflection in theology." [8] Finally, we call attention again to Gustavo Gutierrez, who—as already said—defines theology as critical reflection on praxis. He says that from now on "wisdom and rational knowledge will more explicitly have ecclesial praxis as their point of departure and their context." [9] He says this is a new way to do theology, because it begins with a "protest against trampled human dignity, in the struggle against the plunder of the vast majority of people, in liberating love, and in the building of a new, just, and fraternal society." [10]

We could be led astray, however, if we yielded to the suggestion that theology is only falling for another modernism by turning to the Marxist stress on praxis. I believe the profounder interpretation is that Marxism is providing the challenging occasion for theology to dig more deeply into its own biblical sources for a Christian doctrine of praxis. In my view, philosophy has a perennial task to perform for theology. It performs it best, not by offering up a rival natural theology, but by driving theology to perform more faithfully on its own playing field, to be true to its own originating thematic. It is no mere coincidence that the theology which has been most open to the Marxist theory of praxis is precisely the one which begins with the biblical theme of eschatology. Joining the two terms together, eschatology and praxis, we could say that biblical religion is essentially a matter of "eschatopraxis." The Fourth Gospel speaks of "doing the truth." Biblical truth is eschatological, yet it is something to be done here and now. This calls for action to transform the present for the sake of the oncoming power of the truth. Marxism may be the present-day medium of this new theological doctrine of praxis, but its source is the eschatological message of the Bible.

The positive turn to praxis in theology is being encouraged by other philosophical movements besides Marxism. Pragmatism is a peculiarly American movement whose very name enshrines the idea of praxis. Pragma and praxis both derive from the same Greek word, *prattein,* meaning "to do." In France, Maurice Blondel's philosophy of action is enjoying a revival. Gregory Baum begins his book, *Man Becoming,* by speaking of the Blondelian shift in theology. This refers to the idea that not the intellect alone is the faculty of access to the real, but truth becomes present only through man's choosing and doing. Likewise, existentialism in its own way is an attempt to go beyond Hegel, by stressing the moment of decision in human existence. *Il faut choisir,* Sartre says. Analytic philosophy also prepares the atmosphere for a higher appreciation of praxis by emphasizing that the meaning of language does not lie in its correspondence to an eternal world of ideas or objects, but lies in its function within a particular context. The meaning of language is tied to *what it does.*

Thus, in all these movements we see a trend toward making philosophy practical. It is not surprising, then, that theology which is breathing the same atmosphere as philosophy would exhibit a parallel tendency to bring its theory down-to-earth, to curb its speculative appetite for treasures of thought that were formerly wasted by relegating them to the heavens, by now taking and cherishing the earthen vessels in which all human actions and meanings are confined.

The Unmitigated Importance of Theoria

We are decidedly in favor of the turn to praxis in theology. But having said that, there is a sense in which we are unwilling to abandon the notion of the priority of *theoria*. It is perhaps useful to pause awhile for some elemental distinctions. Theory can have two meanings. When we say *theoria*, we point to its meaning as vision, which is an ingredient in the original Greek concept. When we say theory, we more commonly have in mind its function as explanation. Theory as explanatory is post-practical; it presupposes the existence of facts and actions which call for explanation. Theory as vision, however, is pre-practical; it is prior to every human decision or action. It is not causal explanation but alluring persuasion. If we stress the priority of theory over praxis, we have in mind the mental function of anticipation which is the prius of every meaningful act. Frequently, however, the idea of theory connotes idle speculation and arid intellectualism, unrelated to the concrete events of human existence. In that case, we are referring to the explanatory function of theory which may seem extremely remote from the practical affairs of people who live in the real world.

As we have distinguished two aspects of theory, so also we must draw a distinction between practice and praxis. Practice may refer to whatever is going on as human activity, proceeding from any level of consciousness. Praxis, on the other hand, contains an additional meaning, namely, the power of criticism at work in transforming history and society in order to make human life more human. In light of these distinctions, it is clear that Marx was striving to replace the traditional concept of theory and practice with a new critical theory of praxis. When Karl Marx complained that philosophers have only interpreted the world, he referred to the purely explanatory aspect of theory, which leaves the world just as it is. Then, he added, the point is to change it. For that the visionary aspect of *theoria* is indispensible. There is an element of utopian hope in Marx which cannot be denied and without which there could be no source of criticism at all at the level of praxis. When theory becomes divorced from praxis, that is, when it drifts into a cloud of speculation, it becomes ideology, and ceases to have a critical edge cutting into reality to change it.

Karl Marx charged that theology up to his time had presented itself as theory, and therefore also as ideology, reflecting but not transforming the existing world of facts. It is this critical element in the Marxist theory of praxis that liberation theology has adopted. It would be erroneous to suppose, however, that this alone would make it more practical than other theological approaches. A Marxist philosopher or a liberation theologian may have a splendid theory about praxis oriented to change, revolution and what not, and still sit in an ivory tower of his own. Furthermore, none of the great theological systems that has gone before detached itself from practice. In fact, the notion of theology as a *habitus practicus* goes back at least to the medieval schoolmen, and Luther surely used it to open up a keg of dynamite.

But what about our great teachers of the past generation of theology—Barth, Bultmann, and Tillich? Did they also link theory to praxis in this critical sense? The liberation theologians tend to stress the novelty of their concept of praxis in theology. But is it altogether novel? Is there sheer discontinuity between liberation theology which lays claim to this Marxist notion of praxis and our theological forerunners?

It is one of the merits of Friedrich-Wilhelm Marquardt's book on Karl Barth, *Theologie und Sozialismus,* to have pointed out that the category of praxis, and particularly its relation to theory, played an eminent role in Barth's earliest socialist period. In the first edition of the *Römerbrief* Barth makes clear that correct thinking, rightly understood, is the principle of transformation, making way for something new over against the old world.[11] Even when Barth is writing his *Church Dogmatics* he does not leave the field of praxis. For here theology is understood as critical reflection on the actual proclamation going on in the church, an inquiry into all its presuppositions and implications.[12]

Similarly, it can be argued that Tillich also in his early period of "religious socialism" encountered and incorporated certain Marxist elements into his thought, particularly its critique of ideology and its ethics of social change.[13] Even in writing his *Systematic Theology,* he emphasized in the very first sentence that theology is a function of the church, serving its concrete needs. I think less of a case can be made for Bultmann's theology, although his definition of faith as radical obedience in concrete experience would indicate that for him the answers to the questions of what to do and what is right cannot be deduced from an absolute dogmatics.

It is clear that I would minimize the gap between dialectical theology and liberation theology on the relation between theory and praxis. Barth and Tillich were aware of the ideological tendencies in theology and countered them through principles of criticism deeply rooted in their theological vision. On the other side, they may still have something essential to say to liberation theologians who tend to adopt Marxist rhetoric in an uncritical way. Marx was so eager to go beyond Hegel that he announced the abolition of philosophy in the name of a critical praxis. This notion has its theological analogue in a slogan sometimes heard among enthusiasts of liberation theology that "German academic theology is dead." This slogan is hyphenated with glowing trust in words about praxis, as though now praxis could be the new magic key to the salvation of the world.

A theological critique of praxis will make itself credible only by being more critical than Marxist theory has proved capable of becoming. Wherever Marxist theories have been historically implemented, they have become frozen into a new ideology. A criticism of praxis and of its presuppositions, not only in terms of epistemological theory but also in terms of sociological context, taking into account such factors as whose praxis, in whose interest, and with what effects on the real struggles for freedom and justice, requires the presence of a self-relativizing *theoria*. In pointing to God, theology has in mind the source of all power to criticize and relativize the plans and performances of human agents.

In contrast to the Marxist concept of historical materialism, according to which salvation emerges out of the mute course of history through the revolutionary praxis of the proletariat, I would support a historical idealism which locates the motor for change in the positive symbols of the future which sustain and drive a people forward. I am not optimistic about a movement that seeks to go so far beyond Hegel that it becomes wholly cynical of the power of theory, concepts, doctrines and systems. Only through theory, vision, utopia or eschatology can we hold open the distance between the "is" and the "ought," between description and prescription, between fact and value. During his student years at Tübingen, Hegel and his two friends, Schelling and Hölderlin, adopted an interesting password: "May the Kingdom of God Come." [14] This was their farewell greeting, indicating that in those early years they were not reconciled to the world as it is. They believed in the power of their ideas to change the world, by mirroring things as they are in a picture of how they ought to be. Theory and ideas are not only epiphenomena of a history that generates salvation out of itself. If it was once erroneous to think that theory by itself—or the philosopher's brain—could be the lever of salvation, so now it is equally foolish to imagine that praxis by itself—or the proletariat revolution—will bring about the salvation of the world.

I mentioned the password of Hegel and his friends, because I believe that it points to the biblical basis for a Christian doctrine of praxis. It was Max Stirner who asked the question, "But why ought we change the world?" [15] This question cannot be answered at the level of praxis alone. It was the Jewish vision of the kingdom of God which led to the urgent appeal for repentance. "Repent, for the kingdom of God is at hand." The experience of evil in the world does not of itself justify a belief that the world can or should be changed. It is the intervention of a contrasting vision with inherent power and truth which bestirs the conscience to revolt against the way things are and which generates hope for better things to come.

I stated that theology has good reason not to abandon the notion of the priority of *theoria*. From our theological perspective, Christian praxis is not merely a matter of intuiting the right thing to do on the spot; rather, it is motivated by hope that strains forward to the coming of God's kingdom. Immanuel Kant said that there are basically three categories of human questions. The first is, What can I know? It is a theoretical question. The second is, What ought I do? That is a practical question. The third is, What may I hope? That is both a theoretical and a practical question. Or we could say, it contains both a cognitive and an existential element, something for the mind, something for the will. The hope we are talking about is a total hope that concerns the well being and future being of all that I am. It includes the next step, the next to the last step and the final step that I shall take. In this there is a unity of Christian vision and action.

There are other reasons that praxis presupposes *theoria*.

Christian praxis derives from the liberating power of the gospel; this gospel can be expressed in praxis only when it has first been grasped through faith—a faith which embraces both knowledge and wisdom. This is a gospel that comes *to* us before it finds its way *through* us; it can be *handed on* only because it has been *handed down.* The roots of faith, hope and love are grounded in the soil of the gospel in history. By the power of the Spirit they become fruitful in action. The knowledge of roots precedes the fruits of faith. For this reason the Reformation tradition has relentlessly tried to keep praxis in the second position. The primacy has been reserved for the Word and the faith engendered by the hearing of the Word. Thus, in thinking through the relation between theory and praxis, our theory has a reference not only to what we choose and do, but also to what we know and believe. We have usually expressed this by saying that dogmatics precedes ethics. They must never be separated; but surely the horse should come before the cart. In an eschatological theory of praxis the initiative lies with the power of God and his kingdom breaking into the world, calling for repentance and liberating the will to make things new.

Theory and Praxis in Field Education

Today, a theological school has good reason to withstand an open hostility to theoretical activity and a hasty devaluation of its achievements in favor of a subordination to the requisites of immediate praxis and its tyrannizing adhocracy. This is particularly important when the "now generation" that has insisted on immediate gratification of instincts and feelings comes of age. It has been shown through psychological studies that many of the student activists joined the movement, not because they were guided by any transcendent vision but simply to release aggressive feelings. That is what weekend revolutionaries needed; long-range revolutionaries require something more to keep them going—a transcendent vision that works as a critical guide in the development of praxis.

As we turn to the meaning of these reflections on theory and praxis, as they apply to the practical tasks in the making of a minister, the last thing that I would offer is a new program and a new method. I would attempt a more modest task of putting certain questions to what we are doing.

First of all, I would ask whether I am right in suspecting that an ideology of professionalism offers the governing paradigm in field education. We hear a lot of talk about professional competencies and professional skills. It goes without saying that such things are important. Every artist needs a bag of tools. On the other hand, a musician may learn how to compose, but that does not put music in his head.

I think the notion of the ministry as a profession is theologically ambiguous. Is it not rather a *calling* that syngergizes divine and human dimensions? My question is whether the theological dimension is aggressively applied as the weapon of criticism in the process of professionalizing ministerial training.

Secondly, I would ask whether pouring more of our energies into the professionalizing of the ministry is the best possible therapy for the much ballyhooed crisis of the ministry. As professionalization goes on, the image of the minister gets fuzzier. Defining the minister in terms of what the people want done makes him only the captive flunkie of the status quo; defining him as an agent of social change soon puts him out of a job. We need a theological doctrine of the ministry by which we can decide whether winning or losing, whether success or failure, is better under the present conditions of church life in America. There are times when you can only win by losing; that is the lesson of the cross in history. Nietzsche said there has been only one Christian, and he died on a cross. Jesus was the world's biggest loser and somehow salvation is linked to that event in world history.

I wonder if it is not in the long run dangerous to give to the church a whole generation of ministers equipped with a bag of tricks, when they lack a clear theological self-understanding of their calling as ministers of a message not of their own making. Instead, we often hear some vague talk about ministers being enablers and facilitators. Sören Kierkegaard wrote about the difference between Jesus and Socrates, also about the difference between a good Socratic teacher and an apostle. Socratic education is maieutic; the minister of the gospel is doing something else than mid-wifery.

My hunch is that a lot of field education is going on under the supervision of the seminaries without adequate attention to the theology of the ministry as the critical accompaniment in the development of praxis. Schelling once wrote: "The osten-

sible rush from the theoretical to the practical brings about the
same shallowness in action that it does in knowledge." [16] A
sound theology of ministry alone can orient the candidate to
his professional training in such a way that he becomes a free
person whose identity is not reducible to the sum total of the
functions he has learned to perform in the interest of existing
structures.

Thirdly, I would ask whether field education is undergirded
by a critical pedagogy of the kingdom. We have called it an
eschatological theory of praxis. Such an orientation is worked
out with reference to a theology of the kingdom of God that
makes both the church and the world the theaters of God's liberating activity, but in ways that need to be differentiated. The
old Lutheran doctrine of the two kingdoms was an attempt to
do just that. I believe that particular doctrine needs a new face.
But even in its old form it is much more useful than the non-
doctrine that is often conspicuous in the making of the ministry.
A pedagogy of the kingdom can be defined as anything that
results in a transformation of reality entailing the humaniza-
tion of man. In this respect it doesn't matter whether such an
activity is done in church or in the world; it can be done any-
where and it must be done everywhere. And it can be done by
anyone—even without specific Christian credentials.

I believe that the theory of education which Paulo Freire has
advanced in his book, *Pedagogy of the Oppressed*,[17] fits hand in
glove with this eschatological theory of praxis. His idea of "conscientization" can be appropriated to test whether real education
is going on or only a kind of training to perform certain functions to perpetuate a system. Conscientization refers to the process
in which responsible subjects achieve a more critical awareness of
the realities which willy nilly shape their lives and of their
capacities to transform structures of domination and oppression.

Freire was kicked out of Brazil because he applied his peda-
gogical methods in a literacy campaign. People became aware
of the wider socio-cultural horizons of meaning related to the
words they learned to read. When the dominating classes per-
ceived the revolutionary implications of the method, they put a
stop to it. Are the principles of this pedagogy relevant to life
in the American church, or only to the situation of the Third
World? It would be naive to call for a direct transposition; our
situation is vastly different. However, there are underlying

assumptions about people and their place in society which are not regionally limited.

Conscientization does not merely mean consciousness; it means *critical* consciousness. It operates to break open a closed society by driving a person beyond its existing boundaries. Now, the same thing can happen within the church. A critical consciousness can drive the Christian beyond the limits of the visible church and its institutional self-interest. That is precisely the aim of the eschatological message of Christianity, with its universal horizon of meaning and destiny that lures the church into a mission embracing the whole world.

The point of education, both in its theoretical and practical aspects, is to actualize the human potential of self-transcendence. Man is an open being, capable of going beyond himself and his immediate situation. The main purpose of field education is to ground the liberating process of education in praxis, and not to supply a fund of practical information and practical techniques. In a world in which everything is changing so rapidly, such information and techniques soon become obsolete. With some reason we used to call the courses we took in the practical field "practically theology." The suspicions of my student years have not yet diminished. What we learned turned out to be either outdated or useless. The formation of the prophetic mind and the pastoral heart is the most urgent task. Most of what goes into that formation has no immediate practical use, but that does not make it impractical. The most practical thing is to acquire the kind of solid theoretical knowledge that applies to a wide number of cases, now and in the future. The case-study method, which on the face of it promises to make our knowledge more practical, will in the long run prove less practical. René Dubos states in *Man Adapting*, "In any given field, the leaders are rarely those who have entered professional life with the largest amount of practical information, but rather those who have breadth of understanding, critical judgment, and especially discipline of learning. The intellectual equipment most needed is that which makes it possible to adapt rapidly to new situations, as they constantly arise in the ever-changing world." [18]

Fourthly, I would ask then whether field education leads to the development of a critical consciousness that knows how to serve the church without being subservient to its egoistic interests and that knows how to share in the liberating process going on in the world without surrendering the role of leadership in the congregations. I am asking whether field education does not make parochial people all the more parochial. It may serve to build up or renew a positive loyalty to the empirical church, and that is laudable, but perhaps too many naive myths about this church have to be swallowed in the bargain. I have noticed that the leadership of the empirical church trembles whenever its praxis is subjected to relentless criticism. There is the secular criticism of the church that comes from the world; not even this should be dismissed. And there is a transcendent criticism that stems from the gospel of the kingdom of God. For the church to squelch the voice of prophecy in its own midst leads to self-destruction as the church of the gospel. Paul Tillich stated that the church is different from the world insofar as it is the place where the Protestant principle is kept alive. This is the source of a criticism that regenerates the church through the message of the cross. I don't think there is much theology of the cross in getting people tooled up for institutional ministry. Models of adaptation and growth are prevalent. There is no cross in a world where everybody is okay. We are afraid of intentionally promoting a critical consciousness because we fail to distinguish that from a subversive mentality.

It is possible to distinguish three types of consciousness that prevail in the modern church. The first is a church-centered thinking—ecclesiocentrism. The second erupted in secular Christianity—the church was asked to catch up to the world. We tried that for awhile, lost some members, and now a backlash has set in. I believe we are heading back to a church-centered point of view. But there is a third type—the gospel of the kingdom of God that generates a common horizon of meaning and destiny for the church and the world. That is the source of a critical consciousness that intends to go beyond producing loyal churchmen. Any pedagogy whose highest goal is to produce mere *churchmanship* has little in common with the *ecclesia* of the New Testament.

A critical pedagogy of the kingdom will be characterized by a solidarity with all people, and not only the private group of one's racial, ethnic, cultural or religious origin. It will, furthermore, remove the mythical halo that surrounds the venerated authority which has eclipsed the freedom of the gospel in one's particular church. A critical attitude, if it is kept warm by the fire of the

Spirit, may be a sign of spiritual health, although it will often be mistaken as a form of psychological sickness. Modern psychoanalytic studies of the life of Jesus and of Paul view them largely as sick men. It does not go without saying that their followers should fare any better. Yet, we have found even in theological schools a worshipful attitude toward the results of the psychological testing programs to which candidates for ministry have been subjected. Since I began teaching fifteen years ago, I have witnessed a decrease of confidence in the validity of any theological test for ministry, and an increase of reliance on psychological criteria for ministerial competence. One possible interpretation of this is that the church is looking for healthy people who fit into its ready-made system.

Concluding Words

It would be misleading to leave the impression that my critical remarks would apply exclusively to field education. I believe a similar positivism, in alliance with a professionalism and a parochialism, can be detected throughout theological education.

I do not see any response to the crisis in ministry that arouses a great deal of confidence in either students, professors, or pastors. The most promising initiatives are in a minority position. In the church they will be wracked up on a cross and placed on a hill outside the gate.

Meanwhile, the old values in ministry are not finding the new forms which we thought we could promise and deliver to the church. Preaching is becoming a lost art; the kergyma suffers. Teaching has become group process; the didache does not get passed on. Worship, with all the new liturgies, has become people touching people, but not a more likely occasion for the experience of the holy—the *mysterium tremendum et fascinosum.* Counseling has limped from one psychological approach to the other, because of its wobbly theological legs. At times one fears there is no theology in it at all, no theological doctrine of man to guide the appropriation of psychological insights and methods. Religious education has become a theological desert and evangelism produced the fiasco of Key 73.

The greatest single obstacle to a reunification of theological theory and church praxis is the existing separation of disciplines in our teaching without having a common framework of theo-

logical interpretation to unite them. Pluralism is a good thing;
I am not for uniformity. However, what is done in field education is largely under the control of non-theological methodolo-
gies. Often, the experiential result is theologically alienating. A
fool's dichotomy develops between what is referred to as "academic theology," good for nothing except to keep professors busy,
and practical theology which is often no theology at all, but only
tidbits of psychology or sociology. What we are witnessing is a
kind of methodological anarchy. Attention to the world of objects and to conceptual ideas is blanketed by a sovereign goo of
gut-level feelings. Each individual becomes the pope of his own
feelings. From this anarchic individualism we may quite easily
move into a conformist collectivism in the church. The autono-
my of the one is as bad as the heteronomy of the other.

It may be that those who are on the frontline of field education
will be the first to detect that something is radically wrong. Perhaps they will be the first to call for a reconciliation of theory
and praxis on a theological model. Perhaps they will find new
structures, not only to get students to learn their skills in the
parish setting—an important step forward from the way it used
to be done—but also to make theology the critical guide in the
development of praxis. Field education will not become practical
until praxis becomes theological. Theology is the most practical
thing a student can learn, not only in school but in the field.
The purpose of grounding theology in field work is to test its
claim to truth and its power to guide the church in the way of
light and life. The experiential horizon of practical consciousness
will become secularized the moment it becomes autonomous. The
only hope and justification for field education in a theological
curriculum is for the biblical, hermeneutical, historical, dogmatic
and systematic disciplines to find the right points of re-entry
into the field. I think this is also essential to make them vital
operations in the mediation between theory and praxis.

10

The Social
Perspective of
the Church

This chapter will develop a perspective on the church's involvement in the social sphere. Perhaps it is not necessary to warn in advance not to expect too much from theology in this area. Mostly the church has gotten involved in social welfare out of practical necessity, not because of any clear theological guidelines laid down in advance. Nor should we expect a blueprint from theology, specifying what to do and how much to do in this or that field. Nevertheless, it may be that theology ought not neglect to contribute its little mite to a critical review of the church in social welfare activities.

In recent years the frontline thinking of theology has dealt with politics and protests and the challenges of the hard revolution. In the process the soft revolution, the more quiet ministry of mercy, has proceeded without headlines. This is the caring function of the church. In the total work of modern welfare, what the church does is itself but a widow's mite, if you can talk about a few millions of dollars. The question is whether the church has any real business in the work of social welfare. Why not leave it to the state, which is pledged to care for the life, liberty and the pursuit of happiness of all its citizens? That becomes a theological question! Whatever the practical reasons for having gotten involved in social welfare in the past, is it an essential element of the church's nature to do so? Or is it a take it or leave it proposition? Listen to the words of one of the most prominent theologians in the world today—Wolfhart Pannenberg:

"The specifically social activities of the Church (its welfare organizations, child care centers, nursing and hospital establishments, schools, etc.), are subsidiary and temporary. The Church engages in these activities as a substitute for the political community. The Church's effort should be directed toward making the state ready and able to assume these responsibilities which are appropriate to the political structures of society. It is a strange twisting of its sense of mission when the Church becomes jealous of the state and wants to monopolize certain welfare activities. The Church's satisfaction is in stimulating the political community to accept its responsibilities."

According to this statement, we could perhaps foresee the time when the church can withdraw from the work of welfare and do its proper job of mediating to each individual the awareness of the ultimate mystery of life, by preaching the gospel of God and of his Son Jesus Christ.

The Biblical Basis

In one sense the church never intended to get into the business of social welfare. In the early church there was an intense eschatological consciousness which looked for the end of the world in the near future. There were no long range plans, only the glowing expectation that the Son of man was coming soon. But it did not happen so soon; and it has not happened yet. History is still going on, and that is something the earliest Christians never expected; and there is good evidence to believe that Jesus did not figure it that way either. The early church looked forward to the coming of the kingdom of God and the establishment of his righteousness, and instead found itself becoming fully involved in the ambiguous affairs of world history. As the final advent of the Lord kept being postponed, so that the first generation of Christians gave way to a second, and then to a third, it soon became evident that Christians would have to start digging in for the long and bitter struggles of world history, with its unmitigated suffering and pain, sickness and death. That is how it came about that the church got involved in social welfare. It was an emergency measure, quite out of line with the eschatological time-table of the first Jesus people, but it became inevitable as the church took a few long strides into world history.

First it happened in a simple way. The first deacons were chosen by the apostles to do chores; they were practical-minded people, who tended to the menial duties in the budding community, like waiting on tables, calling on the sick, visiting old people and widows, caring for the orphans, feeding the poor, and administering relief to any person in a time of trouble. John Mackay, former president of Princeton Theological Seminary, once said that the two great focal symbols of Christianity are the cross and the towel—the cross for the saving death of Jesus and the towel for the service done in his name. The deacons were the church's arms of mercy, going about doing good, relieving suffering and drying tears.

A Historical Perspective

How often do we consider that hospitals were a Christian invention? The dark sub-cellars of human misery have been illuminated by Christians bearing the torches of mercy. In England this same mercy drove John Howard into prison reform. In Germany Johann Wichern established a rescue home for neglected children, and Bodelschwingh founded homes for epileptics at Bielefeld. The church was in the vanguard doing educational work among black people before the state cared. Always a few sisters of mercy were there to work among the Indians, long before it became a favorite cause of a Marlon Brando or a Jane Fonda. The church has pioneered the soft revolution, the ministry of mercy among the poor, the left outs and the drop outs—orphans, destitute children, sick people, feebleminded and insane people, alcoholics, prisoners, the aged and so forth. The hard revolutionaries often cry down this work of mercy as having something evil in it. The point the hard core revolutionaries are making is that all these charity institutions are leaving untouched the basic underlying causes producing wretchedness and misery. In fact, the church's works of mercy can help prolong the life of wicked social structures by relieving the pain of their most conspicuous casualties. The very method used guarantees longer life to the structures that produce social disease; that is the method of institutionalization. The unhealthy and insane are conveniently packed away and rendered invisible to the healthy members of society, thus drugging the body into social stupor and high toleration of social wickedness that makes cripples and victims of the weaker members.

The purpose of institutionalization, of course, is to show mercy to those who are sick, insane, retarded, or old, but the way it works is something else again. Institutionalization allows the social body to continue in the illusion that it is basically sound, and that a few works of mercy can make up for the malfunctioning of this or that part of the whole. So the stench of human misery is kept far away from the nostrils of our daily life, so that there is nothing to generate indignation against the evils that cause it.

It used to be, before the modern age, that poverty was essentially an individual phenomenon. The poor could be cared for one by one. Institutions could be created to handle unfortunate individuals more efficiently. No thought was given to social causes. This was before the age of sociology. A poor man was seen as an unlucky individual, or perhaps as lazy, and thus, as they say, "having it coming to him." The church also looked at individual drop-outs in this individualistic way, taking no initiative to treat each sick person as a part mirroring the truth about the whole. With the coming of the modern age this individualistic outlook will not do. Each case is tied to a cause rooted in the collective whole. "We are members one of another." We are not Robinson Crusoes each on his own little island. We are part of the social lump. Each case cries out for social cure. In modern social pathology the biblical maxim is borne out: "If one member suffers, all suffer together" (1 Cor. 12:26). Perhaps the last group in modern society to accept the sociological implications of this, besides the Daughters of the American Revolution, is the church.

Mass suffering is a social phenomenon, and no solution which tackles the problem piece-meal, in bits and pieces, putting each victim on a stretcher and carrying him away into an institution designed for him and his kind, has any long range validity. It may appear like the merciful thing to do in the emergency situation, but, I repeat, it has no positive long range validity. The man who cradles the victim's head in his arms must turn around and point the accusing finger in the right direction, and say, "Look what you have done!" When the Christian church, in caring for the suffering, begins to see what causes the suffering, and speaks out on what it sees, its mercy will be coupled with anger, and its ministry will become a double force in society, using the right hand to love the individual victims with all the resources at its command, and the left hand closing into a clenched fist as a symbol of resolve to change the system that produces needless suffering.

The Contemporary Dilemma

But there is a contemporary dilemma. The social perspective is holistic. It means that the individual cases of suffering and defeat are defects in the total social system. So nothing less than a total package can integrate the odds and ends back into the social organism. This triggers a drive to have comprehensive solutions to all the problems. The result is the modern welfare state, at first appearing on the horizon as a rainbow sign of great hope, that at last we have found a universal father to care for us poor children all the way from the cradle to the grave. But there behind the rainbow a dark cloud is forming which may soon, if it has not already, burst upon us, showering us not with blessings from on high, but with fire and brimstone from the wrath of God in heaven. The social liberals wanted a comprehensive welfare state born from a generous humanitarian spirit that has its roots in the biblical idea of love for the neighbor and justice for all men. But that same state which was given so much power to become a total welfare state now turns that power to its own advantage in becoming an omnipotent warfare state. This is what is devolving upon us, a total system —we may as well use the filthy word we have reserved for our communist enemies—a totalitarian welfare-warfare state, which may well take us into the world of B. F. Skinner, beyond freedom and dignity, sooner than later—and much too soon for me. I do not think I want to be living in *1984*. I still agree with Socrates: "It is better to be an unhappy man than a contented pig."

This is the dilemma I see. While a few years ago I counted myself among the social liberals, and would have let the state take over all the welfare activities, now I shrink back from that, because I believe that the monopoly of power by one institution is more than man can handle. It is like putting a loaded gun in the hands of a child. It is like putting the power of God in the hands of mortal man and hope that it does not go to his head. Well, the power of the people has gone to the head of the modern state, and now it is acting puffed up, arrogant and indifferent to the cries of its people. Only at election time does it fake a few spasms of concern. My fear used to be that the political powers would make promises to get elected and then would not keep them. Now my fear is that when they make the promises, they really plan to keep them. The universal father will promise to do everything for his child—putting the bottle in his mouth and changing his diapers. That will surely be a life "beyond freedom and dignity."

When the church reviews what business it has in the field of social welfare, it must be clear about the total context. It cannot make a good decision by consulting its private feelings. It must read the signs of the times, and know where it is at in the world of history—political, social, economic history as a whole.

A Suggestion for Now

We cannot say that Christian theology has a doctrine of social welfare for all seasons, the same in every time and place. In essential terms we might agree that welfare is the business of the state, and that the church is in it only on a temporary basis, as a substitute for the state. But in fact the church will be in the business of welfare for a long time to come and perhaps for the duration of history. In essential terms we could say that if the state were fully doing its job and doing it well, all the church would have to do is deal with ultimate reality, the ultimate mystery of life that grounds and mediates the final meaning of life. The church could, in other words, stick to its purely religious business. But in fact it does not work out that way. For the state does not do its job well enough, never has and never will. The church will always have to go beyond its proper function of preaching the Word, and seek as much earthly cash value for that Word of life in the world in which people are living their death ahead of time. For the death which all people die is working retroactively, seeking to claim the lives and loyalties of people from the cradle to the grave. So death gets paid off ahead of time, unless the Word of life is thrown into battle all along the line.

One reason for the church to stay in the business of welfare is to counter the omnipotence of the welfare state. It must set up a shield against the tendency of the state to penetrate every sphere of life, and control the care of children, the sick, the insane and the aged. The power of the universal father must be balanced by the heart of the caring mother. So another reason that the church must stay in the business of welfare is that although the state can supply the material and the technology of caring for people in need, it has no message that cares for the inner man, that gives profound meaning to life. Whenever the state tries to invade the sphere of the inner man, it becomes ideological and demonic, and must be resisted to the bitter end, as Bodelschwingh did to the Hitler state when he refused to put into practice the Nazi racist theory on eugenics. The church belongs to welfare, because the most overwhelming apparatus of care in the world is not good enough if it leaves out the direct personal touch of love to neighbor and the dimension of meaning for the inner man. The church has the message rooted in the personal nature of love and the ultimate mystery of life. The omnicompetent state will be handling the volume of business it will be getting in welfare, a volume which is linked somehow to its growing volume of business in warfare, in terms of cases. Persons become cases in a mechanized and computerized state system. The word "case" comes from the Latin *casus,* meaning "fall." A case is a person who has fallen into the dehumanizing machinery of the welfare state. If the church does not stay in the business of welfare, the state will take over also the function of the church to minister to the inner man, and become a pseudo-church, generating the idolatry of state religion.

A third reason for the church to stay in the business of welfare is better to attack the causes that make it necessary. None of the great utopias have ever made provision for a special welfare agency. Why not? Because the conditions of utopian existence are not causes of poverty and misery. Now, although we do not believe a utopia is coming round the corner, we do not fatalistically conclude that nothing can be done to change things. The church is to accept the poor, but hate poverty, and declare war on the conditions that cause it. If there is something in the American way of life that makes it inevitable for twenty percent of its people to live in dismal poverty, then we must oppose it. The words of Isaiah apply: " 'What do you mean by crushing my people, by grinding the face of the poor,' says the Lord God of hosts" (Isa. 3:15).

The works of mercy are not enough. The church may be generous in its gifts to missions and to charities, but if it does not enter into the clash to change the conditions that make men miserable, in flop houses, prison cells and mental wards, it is not enough. The church must be like its Lord who, though he was rich, became poor for our sakes. Then welfare becomes a two-pronged activity, a friendly hand to those who have stumbled and a thorn in the flesh of the existing establishment. Who is fit to enter the lists of public criticism, if not the church? Who has a right to speak out if not those who hear the sobs of pain in the outcast and the downcast whom others speed by unheeding?

The fourth reason is that every society needs a pioneering group to search out new pockets of misery in the hidden underground of life. Lots of people thought the Indians were okay on their reservations. My aunt never could understand why my mother went to the mission field, because as she was wont to say, "Aren't all the heathen happy in their own religion?" People thought that old people were being well cared for in the nursing homes. People believed the retarded children in New York had good institutional care, until a roving reporter ran in with his cameras and shocked the nation by the pictures he took. The church must stay in welfare, so it can be like that roving reporter, and say, "There is a deep well of tears here, hidden behind the walls of these tomb-like institutions." Ten percent of children in America are on welfare. Who will plead their cause?

This last Christmas a much talked about book came out entitled, *The Death of Christmas.* It was written by two persons concerned about the plight of the needy in Chicago, to help raise money for the Neediest Children's Christmas Fund. The goal of this fund was one Christmas present for every needy child in Chicago. I read the book and applauded the concern of its authors and their goal to bring a little of the joy of Christmas to the poor children of Chicago. But I also felt sick to my stomach. The same old story, I thought, taking up a collection for the poor. This is the church's bag and they will fall for it, pretending that a little Christmas candy can sweeten the bitter pills of poverty. The same old story, I thought, calling on private charity to answer social disease, personalistic answers to public problems. Crumbs falling from the master's table.

Perhaps what we are saying is that in social work, too, an ounce of prevention is worth a pound of cure. Every inch of improvement has to be fought for. People do not by nature really care about their neighbors. Humanity is not just going to roll into the millenium. There is no natural drift to social awareness and self-sacrificing action. People must be made to see and to care. People must be made to see what is wrong and put a stop to it. That is a tough uphill battle. If in the past the church's welfare role has been as caretaker of those evicted from society, for whatever reason, now and in the future the church must give equal attention to prophetically preventive activity. In crass economic terms, this might mean that for every dollar spent on social mercy, another has to be spent on social prophecy. This will involve social research undergirding social preaching calling for social righteousness. Within our welfare societies the church will have its own counterpart to "Nader's Raiders," exercising its own social conscience, practicing its own prayer for humanity, making its own exposés of the structures that hide their tyranny behind a mask of patriotism.

Finally, I think it necessary to warn against a care-less disregard for the Christian character of the church's involvement in welfare activity. The spirit of the times is dictating a self-defeating kind of tolerance which makes the church an easy victim of secularism. It is at work in all the church's auxiliaries, including its colleges and agencies. According to this spirit the church is guilty of discrimination and zealotry if it insists on Christian commitment and articulateness on the part of those who represent its services in the world. I am ashamed to see how often Christians, even in high posts of leadership, are themselves ashamed of the implications of the gospel truth they profess to believe and have to declare. There will be a trend toward the infiltration of the ranks of the army of Christian social workers by fifth columnists, who mean to do good and serve people, but who do not share the faith of Jesus Christ. This will bring about a further weakening of the Christian witness in the world, an erosion of faith, a diminishment of the sacrificial spirit, because people will be in it for the job. And a job is a job. It is exchangeable for another job, a better job. But no vocation, no calling.

The church has an ordained ministry, but no real concept of the structural significance of the diaconate as part of the church. We have had deacons and deaconesses, but apparently we have no significant recovery of the diaconate as Luther tried to do. The troubles ahead in the areas of social ministry and social welfare, lying as they do in the public realm and not in the inner liturgical life of the church, are tied up with the anemic condition of the diaconate. We must not allow our social work to be secularized, but go on to develop a diaconate for works of mercy and ministry to structures such as the church has never had to create in her past history.

11

Untimely Reflections on Women's Liberation

The rabbit has become the symbol of America's obsession with sex. Many beautiful bodies aspire to become *Playboy's* mate of the month, and failing that, to enter the stable of bunnies in Hefner's harem. The women's liberation movement has rightly attacked the image of the female in *Playboy* philosophy. The bunny is the symbol of the sexual exploitation of women by men. It means depersonalization—the reduction of a person to a body whose chief function is to stimulate the sexual glands of the male.

It is easy to share the indignation of the women's liberation movement when the target is the *Playboy* phenomenon. But the movement goes much farther than that. The goal is apparently a completely new place for women in society. When the demand for liberation is expressed in *total* terms and the rhetoric becomes revolutionary, many of us become nervous. As men we naturally become defensive. We like to think that our wives are already happy. But housewives also become fidgety. The women's liberation people make it sound as though a woman has to have an important career to be liberated. Many married women feel they are looked down upon as "mere housewives." If a woman is happy being a wife and a mother, there must be something wrong with her head.

What is it that the women's liberation people want? How far should the movement go? Are there any norms or guidelines? This chapter will be an attempt to offer a theological perspective on women's liberation. There are some real values at stake without regard to which the liberation movement can result in the diminishment of both men and women, the devaluation of sex, love, marriage, and the parental role. Before we spell out—from a theological point of view—the conditions under which the liberation movement ought to proceed, we offer a few more preliminary observations on current ambiguities in the movement.

First of all, women's liberation is a misnomer. There can be no liberation of women without the liberation of men. It is not the case that the liberation of women will cost men some of their freedom. They will become free together or not at all. Women's liberation sometimes implies that men are already free; women want only to go where freedom is. So they go to work. Of all the odd ideas, this is the oddest—freedom is getting a job. But it could be that to go where the men are is for most women only to enter the slave market, and bitterly to discover their men in "chains." Perhaps then we can have a new movement—human liberation. That would be freedom from the curse of a job that you really hate, freedom from the indignities you suffer to bring home a paycheck, the bulk of which is spent anyway on keeping the woman at work, what with baby sitting, maid service, car fare, lunch downtown, clothes in style, etc., etc. If women's liberation has nothing better to offer than to lure women into the job market, nothing has been accomplished to free people from the false consciousness that work defines the dignity of a person. It only reveals how hung-up women's liberation is on the work ethic of our Protestant past.

Secondly, women's liberation can be a trap for those who substitute attendance at women's liberation meetings in place of doing something liberating in the world. Some talk about it, others do it. There are many openings for both men and women in volunteer organizations that contribute to the movement of human liberation—peace groups, anti-pollution campaigns, civil rights, alternatives in education, political criticism—none of which can promise a paycheck at the end of the week. Money or career can be a gauge of justice in society, but never of liberation. Women should have the same chance as men in making money and building careers, but who wants to call that liberation?

Thirdly, women should project a new image of their role in society, imaginatively different from the male role at the present time. This is not yet coming through. Either we hear the negative side; they do not want to be stuck at home, doing housework, changing diapers, and feeling bored and useless. Or we hear the positive side; their goal of liberation is to get equality with men. But that will only bring justice, not freedom. That will only qualify them to share equally with men the burdens, miseries and humiliations they suffer in the world. There are very few men who do not hate their work, very few who get paid for doing what they really enjoy. Otherwise, why the clamor for higher pay, shorter hours, softer conditions, etc.? Otherwise, why all the ulcers, the heart attacks, the lower life-expectancy, etc.? A really new role for women could also mean more liberation for men—an increase of freedom for all.

Sex

Women's liberation is sensitive about sex. As the blacks speak about racism, they speak about sexism. Both are right. Our society is racist and sex-saturated. The analogy is perfect. Both classes are oppressed in terms of every public measuring stick— income, ranks, promotions, opportunities, etc. But the analogy should be carried further. The blacks have come to realize that there is hope in their difference. But at least one vociferous trend in women's liberation is to press for sameness. The blacks went through that stage once; integration was the aim, to show they are the same. But now, "black is beautiful." That is liberation. Some of the louder women in the movement have not come that far. They run down the difference. They are not yet liberated enough to say, "Woman is beautiful!" That sounds too much like a male chauvinist slogan.

I think the theological tradition does have something to say about sexuality that cannot be ignored in any liberation movement. It is possible to blaspheme the Creator by degenerating the dignity and goodness of human sexuality in its differentiation between male and female. The French say, "Vive la différence!" That is not a mere joke; it is a biblical concept. When God creates man in his own image, he does not create a solitary sexless individual, but male and female in their sexual difference. A single human being by himself could not reflect the image of God, unless God were a static unity. But God has revealed himself as essentially love, and love is not a static thing. Love presupposes difference and generates relationship. To be in love is to open up one's existence to another, as God has opened himself up to humanity in Jesus Christ. Sexuality is to be a servant of relationship in love, of driving men and women into unity without cancelling their enjoyable difference.

There are two myths about human sexuality. In the biblical myth of Adam and Eve sex is radical. It goes down to the roots of the creative activity of God. In the Platonic myth of the spherical man, uni-sex is the original state. In the beginning there is the hermaphrodite, embracing both sexes in one being, which later split apart into the two sexual halves of mankind. In this myth sexuality is not rooted in creation, but comes about through a kind of fall. The meaning of the biblical myth is that liberation will not happen by overcoming sexual identity and distinctiveness. There is no freedom or future for woman or man in the direction of collapsing the bi-polar nature of humanity. Sexuality is not a source of sin, overcoming it not the way of liberation. There is a little bit of the old gnostic heresy in our culture, so far as it moves toward the de-feminization of woman and the effeminization of man. Liberated women will not give themselves plastic bodies, handing themselves over to a culture that would reduce them to sex objects; nor will they condemn their sexuality, as though they can achieve personal dignity through shapelessness. The loss of sexual consciousness is not a good thing. A woman who is not proud of her sexual uniqueness will soon become shapeless through what she eats and what she wears. I say that is disgusting, even at the risk of being called a "male chauvinist."

Love

Because the sexual factor is an integral part of the image of God mirrored in the polarity of the sexes, it also expresses a profound element in the mystery of human love that achieves intense expression in the "one flesh" union of man and woman. But sex does not exhaust the meaning of love. The reality of love must be stretched out through analysis, so that we overcome the disease of language which tends to collapse the many dimensions of love into the sex drive. It is trite to say, but "love *is* a many splendored thing." We can discern four dimensions of love. The point of mentioning them is to ask, "Is the liberation movement driving with them, or against them?" Only love can create the path to freedom.

What is love? We can read about it in Erich Segal's beautiful best-seller, *Love Story*. I do not care what the critics say, anyone who has been in love knows it is a true story. There is *libido* in it—lots of it between Jennifer and Oliver. *Libido* is Freud's word for the drive that brings a man and a woman into sexual union. It is part of the scheme of things, part of God's creation, and therefore both natural and good. But *libido* like everything else functions in a state of its perversion. Sin is total in scope. Therefore, it expresses itself as egocentric impulse toward infinite pleasure. The problem is that the ecstasy of sex lasts only a few seconds. It is fleeting; but it is also fickle. The other person can become just any body in the economy of *libido*. *Libido* uses the other person to get rid of tensions or to fill a biological desire. So a prostitute—or sometimes an animal—is all the *libido* needs. The *libido* becomes autonomous—a law unto itself. The authentic purpose of *libido* is to generate a deep personal union. Its inauthentic expression is frustration. The Don Juans and Casanovas do not lead their lovers into deep and lasting personal relationships, but leave in their wake a wreckage of human lives.

Can *libido* be personalized? The search for the answer leads to another dimension of love. We will call this *eros*—to use Plato's term. Freud's *libido* needs fulfilling in Plato's *eros*. *Eros* is the type of love generated in one person by the inherent beauty of the other. It is erotic fascination for the sheer loveliness of the other. It includes but goes beyond *libido* in acknowledging the other person in the power of his or her own beauty and goodness. *Love Story* integrates *libido* and *eros*. It is a first-rate romance. Romantic love has gotten a bad press by theologians (Cf. Denis de Rougement's *Love in the Western World* and Anders Nygren's *Agape and Eros*) who are too quick to run down *eros* so that *agape* may abound. *Eros* is the love between Oliver and Jennifer who desire each other as whole persons, not only as a means of mutual sexual stimulation and release.

Unfortunately, *eros* also must express itself under the conditions of sin. Like *libido* it can be fickle, fleeting, and frustrative. Our language is accurate; we speak about "falling in love" and "love at first sight." One cannot do much about it. Therefore, it is sheer stupidity to base marriage on love (as *libido* and *eros*) if you want it to last awhile. There is a strain of anti-marriage thinking in women's liberation. And why shouldn't there be, since marriage in our culture is based on "falling in love"? Who knows how long any love will last? If falling in love is a good enough reason for getting married, then falling out of love is adequate reason for getting divorced. But that can be complicated, so why become entangled in marriage in the first place? The point to be stressed is that *libido* plus *eros* are not enough for marriage. It is one thing to get a man and woman together, quite another to keep them together. Two persons head over heels in love usually possess the irrational belief that *their* love will last forever, so they do not hesitate to make promises that involve a future they cannot foresee. *Eros* can incite a person to make a promise. But what will make him keep the promise? With this question *libido* and *eros* seek fulfillment in another dimension of love beyond themselves.

When *libido* cools off and *eros* loses its spontaneity, there is a power of love to sustain and deepen the personal union of a man and a woman. We will call it by Aristotle's word—*philia*. It means friendship. If *libido* and *eros* do not mature into friendship, the life span of love between two persons will not be long. The frailties of *libido* and *eros* need the strength of companionship. This, more than the easy promises of *eros,* will generate the altruistic virtues of constancy, fidelity and loyalty. *Philia* is more patient and steady. It does not call for instant ecstasy, but an ever-increasing penetration of the virtually inexhaustible mystery of two selves in love with each other. Elderly couples may experience an increase of love, even though the energies of *libido* and *eros* are on the wane. In view of this quality of love —*phila*-love—we have reason to worry when models of liberation are advanced that draw husbands and wives into completely different life-situations. When there was only one career in the family, usually the husband's, the wife could participate vicariously in the fate and fortune of her husband's vocational life. Women's liberation rightly finds that unsatisfactory now, for it has too obviously resulted in the subservience of women.

Since in our society values are attached to dollars, women who do not work lack the means to prove their worth. No wonder that women's liberation can hardly imagine an alternative for a liberated woman in our society than to get a job earning big money. It is the only ticket to heaven. I am surely not saying that women should stay home or that they should find fulfillment exclusively through their husbands. That has been the typical model. The issue is *not at all* whether women work or not, whether they have a fulfilling career or not. What is at stake is the chances of *philia*-love. That is the criterion of real liberation. The quality of *philia*-love is worth a lot more than a self-glorifying career or a pile of money that can purchase empty symbols of self-adoration. *Philia*-love does not grow by itself. It requires that two persons enter the same space-frame and time-frame long enough to find each other and hold to each other through experiences of a mutually entwining kind. In many cases liberation is just another name for the existing alienation of husband and wife. They choose to drift from each other in separating activities because the fulfilling joy of *philia* is lacking in their relationship. Going to work may be the wisest thing to do under the circumstances. But please do not call it liberation. It is only an alternate form of alienation.

All the dimensions of love—*libido, eros, philia*—are poisoned by unrelenting egoism in all persons. Even the best of friends can have a falling out. Thank God, there is another dimension of love, the greatest of them all, the love of forgiveness. This forgiving love came to expression through God's self-giving activity in Christ. The New Testament writers called it *agape*. It is a self-spending suffering love. *Agape* acts in the interest of the other person. It is unselfish and other-directed. When the other loves break down, it perseveres. It is stronger than *philia* and is the polar opposite of *libido*. *Libido* is primarily interested in fulfilling its own desire; *agape* asks about the need of the other. *Libido* is impatient; *agape* quietly accepts the challenge of fulfilling the other person. For this reason husbands, who are not fully engaged in seeking the liberation of their wives under the humiliating conditions of our male-oriented society, are not sensitive to the demands of *agape*. Wives cannot do it by themselves. When they are forced into it, without the support of their husbands, they become aggressive and arrogant, adopting attitudes no less unbecoming to men. They think of liberation in terms of competitiveness, of getting even, of taking men down a notch or two. Along this path women punish themselves in punishing their men. The quest of liberation not carefully guided by the demands of love in its multi-dimensional reality will only lead to new forms of alienation and oppression. Women's liberation does not talk a lot about love. Perhaps they are too busy fighting for liberation. Perhaps they intend to return to the delicate issues of love after they win their freedom and equality with men. Our contention is that women's power can bring justice, as it is doing in all fields, but only love can bring liberation.

Marriage

Hinging liberation to love, not merely to justice, links it most closely to marriage and the family. Together with the dimensions of love, the structures of marriage and family are affected by the liberation movement. As structures they can be experienced as liberating frameworks or as confining strait-jackets. Marriage has been given a hard rap by liberation people. It has been with us so long, especially in its monogamous state, that it seems like old-hat. Perhaps it's even the cause of our problems. There is no doubt that a lot of people put up with marriage in quiet misery. There is no doubt that marriage can be hell when love is absent and terror takes its place. Still, the abuse of marriage does not call for its disqualification. Marriage is, on the contrary, a norm in the quest of liberation for women. We can say with Karl Barth that whatever is compatible with marriage is good and everything is bad that is incompatible. Fulfill your marriage and do as you please! If marriage is getting in the way of women's liberation, then liberation is wrongly conceived or marriage is not realizing its potential. It is important, then, to have clearly in mind what marriage is—from a theological perspective. It is an institution of society—every society. At the same time it is an act of God at work "behind man's back" to create and fulfill the life of humanity. The drives of sex and love are the means God uses to pressure persons or lure them into marriage. God's creative work is done in this entirely natural way. His commandment is heard not so much as a word from above, but as a pressure from below. Men will do the will of God even against their will, because God is a living, active power in every nerve and sinew of man's being. Thus Luther spoke of marriage as a "worldly thing" and at the same time as the work of God the Creator.

It is this vision and experience of marriage as a divine institution, and not merely a matter of social convention or personal convenience, that causes Christians to perk up when they hear wild schemes of liberation violating or superceding the framework of marriage. The end of marriage is an element of the eschatological vision, no doubt. But its cancellation in history is a bit of enthusiasm that Christians will meet with soberness. Why there should be "no marriage in heaven" can only be imagined in terms of something like a total erotization of all persons endlessly without genital restrictiveness. But that prospect blows my mind; so on with marriage for the time being!

It is interesting that the gospel of the kingdom of God does not bring a new order of marriage at all. At most it maximizes the possibilities of life under the existing order of marriage. But it does admittedly point to a future in which the boundaries of marriage will be erased. For the present it affirms marriage as a good thing and adopts it as a sacrament of Jahweh's relation to Israel and Christ's love for his church. But in no way is marriage taken up into a supernatural order so that its validity and meaning pertain to Christians alone. The formal facts of life—of sex and love and marriage—are the same for Christians and non-Christians alike.

There is a widespread cynicism about marriage. It comes in for a lot of derision on talk-shows and in the underground press. Perhaps people are only laughing at their own failures in marriage; perhaps they are striking back at parents whose broken marriages inflicted so much pain on their children. No wonder that the thrust to liberation will include hopes for new styles of marriage. The question is whether there are some continuing determinants in marriage that must accompany the changing shapes. I think there are, and that it is liberating to keep them in mind in the midst of so much normless experimentation with marriage.

First of all, the living God is not on the side of changelessness. There has been a great variety of patterns in the concrete ordering of marriage and family life and there is no reason to expect that the one with which we are most familiar is the last and the best.

Secondly, the history of marriage is not meaningless change without progress. The impact of the gospel on the structure of marriage reveals a wide gap between the intention of God and the failure of man. The gospel sets in motion a new awareness of what marriage can be. It develops a vision of *perfections of marriage* that promise to make life more free, more personal and more communal. These are impulses of the gospel that can enlarge and deepen common human experience.

Thirdly, the promise of life-long union is one such perfection of marriage that we cannot relinquish. The words are: "So long as ye both shall live." Many supposedly liberated people do not like it. How can a person make a promise that so completely ties up his future? There is little doubt that many Christians have gone along with the social trend to make the dissolution of marriage easy and convenient. The content of their promise is then: "So long as ye both shall love." I would think that the Christian faith, so far from swimming with the cultural trends on sex and marriage, would seek to establish its identity as a vigorous countercultural power. Now is the time for Christians to go against the stream, to show that life is lived from promise, and so also in marriage. The promise is unconditionally valid— no strings attached. It is for better or worse and there is no way out. The content of the promise is that the commitment of two persons is not for as long as love lasts. It is for the duration.

Fourthly, monogamy is a perfection of marriage, superior to polygamy (many wives) and polyandry (many husbands). Why is it superior? Because the power of love is so personalizing that it crowds out any third party from the husband-wife relationship. Love requires a life-long commitment to one other person to achieve its deepest personal potential. Western culture has abandoned the meaning of monogamy in favor of serialized polygamy —many wives, one right after the other. When some of the new communes set aside monogamy and members prefer to "sleep around," they are only refusing to be bound by the external form of marriage that the official culture clings to after emptying out the internal content. This hypocrisy understandably gives rise to cynicism in the younger generation.

Fifthly, the monogamous form of marriage has the purpose of making it clear to children who their parents are. No child should have to be ignorant of who his father or mother is, or to have to choose between them. Some modern parents may think it chic for themselves, but no child would ever choose to be a bastard.

Sixthly, if the monogamous marriage is to possess interior meaning, it is essential that the husband and the wife accentuate their sexual difference. An effeminized male is to a woman a poor substitute for a real man. They are supposed to be partners helping each other in their different needs. It takes time and lots of practice to become the sexual playmate the other partner desires. Women are asking for trouble, worse than what they already have, if they try to flee from their sexual role as females to play a masculine role. Men will never be satisfied with women too much like themselves; they would rather find their fulfillment with women who retain their unlikeness—*ex oppositio.*

Family

Finally, the family. Liberation means at least equality of the sexes before the law. The real revolution ahead of us will happen when we take seriously what we have said about sex, love and marriage. That would call for a new type of family situation. That is what I think women are looking for. A woman is not the property of a man, so why should she take his name? She is not the servant of man, so why should she do the servile chores? If I hate them, so does my wife. We should be partners, each one advancing the other's dignity and pursuit of personal fulfillment.

The New Testament does not reinforce the social hierarchy of its day, making the wife subordinate. In fact, the husband loses his alleged right to "lord it over" his wife as a superior. The idea of the superiority of the male is undercut by transposing the question of his relation to the wife from the sociologically determined category of domination to the new christological category of *agape*-love. The husband is to love his wife with the kind of *agape* by which Christ loves his church. This motif of *agape* exerts a polemical thrust against any social order in which women are treated as chattel or objects subject to the decisions of their husbands. This thrust has been the most powerful weapon in the liberation of women, but its work is still incomplete.

A new status for women in society will call for a new relation of husbands to the children. What is needed is a new family system so that women are not shut up in their little boxes all day, with their husbands off to work. Women feel left out and they are crushed by the routine chores around the house. It is the worst conceivable system. And the children suffer in these tightly enclosed nuclear families. The essence of the family is the natural relation between parents and children. It is a fact, not to be ignored, that everyone born has a father and a mother. This fact can be gathered up into innumerable family structurings. Perhaps we need a clustering of families, so that children grow up with single people and elderly people, who can help in rearing the children and serve as a buffer between children and parents, where so much alienation is experienced. Then if one parent dies or abandons the family, the children can fall back on a network of intimate relationships in the supportive community. Children also have a right to a liberation movement. Perhaps that together with the pressures from women's liberation will force some breakthroughs to new collective homes in which families come together to form little communities more fulfilling for all its members. Think of how the older people need it.

All power to the liberation movement—for women, for children and for husbands and fathers too. I have tried to state that liberation will not come through disregard of essential theological-ethical perspectives on sex, love, marriage and the family. The conditions of enslavement in our society from which we seek liberation do not come from an overdose of faithfulness to the Christian vision of love and marriage. Rather, our society is terribly underdeveloped in that regard. Christians should cease going down-stream with our sexually perverted culture, hollow marriages and miserable family life-styles. Perhaps liberation will come only when people are revolted enough to try some drastically new ways of realizing the human potential envisioned in the incomparably high Christian ethic of sex, love, marriage and the family. A clear vision of these goals can keep the liberation movement on the right road, and spare it from foolish deviations and sub-human adventures.

12

Caring for the Future: Where Ethics and Ecology Meet

Introduction

Mankind is facing global disaster in the near future. That is not a prophetic statement from sacred scripture, but a computer prediction reported by a team of M. I. T. scientists. This team has published its now famous report under the unspectacular title, *The Limits to Growth*.[1] This is a study of the future as a blown-up version of the present; it is a future in bondage to the conditions and trends which already exist. It is not the liberated future that lives in dreams, not a visionary future projected by men with their heads in the clouds. It is the matter-of-fact future sketched by scientists with their feet on the ground. Unfortunately, not a single person on earth would care to live in the kind of future they portray. We are given the picture of an exhausted future—exhausted because now we are burning up the fuels of life that belong to coming generations. We are sacrificing the children of tomorrow—indeed, their very existence—on the altars of self-indulgence today.

Scientific predictions, of course, do not decree the future. They are extrapolations from the present into the future. They deal with the empirically probable future, not the morally desirable future. They do not rule out the possible emergence of new factors which might well reverse the current trends leading to global collapse. They do not deny the realm of freedom in history, which is the source of surprises, novelties, miracles and truly revolutionary interventions. Otherwise scientific predictions would render moral decisions meaningless. The meaning of a moral decision presupposes the power of freedom and a still open future. In this chapter I will deal with these two

dimensions in our approach to the future, the scientific and the
ethical, the one telling us what the future is likely to be on the
basis of known data, however horrid and inhumane, the other
moving us to work for a more fulfilling future on the basis of
conscience, no matter how unlikely and implausible. It is in our
approach to the future that our ecological forecasts and our
ethical decisions meet and possibly collide. Morally sensitive
persons will have to become rebels against the scientifically pre-
dicted future for the sake of a morally superior one. We are engaged in a kind of civil war between alternative futures; the
time is becoming desperately short; it is not enough to get our
facts straight; we must try to get our futures sorted out. To cope
with the announcements of ecological damnation on a planetary
scale, we must quickly shift our thinking to the future, to develop a future-oriented ethic. Such an ethic does not merely
reflect back upon the moral dilemmas of the past, deciding the
right and the wrong, the good and the bad, concerning actions
that have already happened. Rather, it looks to the future with
prospective interest, in terms of an anticipatory calculus.

The Ecological Problem

Our educational practice tends to appeal to that aspect of
human nature which prevents us from seeing farther than the
end of our collective noses. Human beings are very interested in
what is coming up next and what is going on immediately
around them. In any culture the people who think in terms of
the far-off future—say, the next 30 to 100 years—and act out of a
global awareness are very few, indeed. The majority of people
care about the next few days, the next few weeks, perhaps about
the next few years, and they care about themselves, their families, their jobs, their neighborhoods, perhaps also the well-being
of their own race and nation, but that is all. They do not look
far ahead in time and they do not really care about what is
happening far away. In terms of the dimensions of time and
space, which set the limits of human existence, we all tend to
live it up big and spend it all in the immediate here and now.
This is true of individuals, of small groups, of nations and their
governments. We repeat, there are very few people who really
care about the future of coming generations and who manifest a
global consciousness.

If we trace the course of human evolution and cultural development to the present time, it has never seemed necessary for people heretofore to possess a future-consciousness and a global perspective in order to survive and thrive. "Sufficient unto the day was the evil thereof." Human survival followed the path of immediate self-interest; each part had only to watch out for itself and that would be good for the whole. Now the reverse is becoming true; there won't be any surviving parts without attention to the future well-being of the whole—the whole of humanity in a world community that is united in the pacification of the earth planet.

The need for a future-consciousness that forms the horizon of a new planetary ethic is bound up with the ecological problem. Not so long ago we were getting mainly good news about what science and technology were doing for mankind. Now we are getting our ears full of bad news about what man and the machines he has made are doing to the earth. Trends have been set in motion that promise to carry away our human future and lay it in a tomb. The trends are widely studied and debated: spreading and accelerating industrialization around the world as the only model for the future on which governments act; continuing the population growth rate in exponential terms; the growing gap between the rich and the poor, the staggering suffering and starvation, the inequitable distribution of goods; then the depletion of the earth's resources in absolute terms; finally, the pollution of the environment, choking off life itself. I am one of those who tend to believe our scientific friends who tell us that if the trends keep curving at their present rate, they will wind the spring in the mechanism of our human future so tight, that it will snap. Human civilization as we know it will die or be disfigured beyond recognition.

I am not concerned in this chapter to offer any new data or assemble any new statistics. The large picture is good enough for me. It shows that we are quite rapidly reaching the outside limits to growth that this finite world system will tolerate, before it lashes back at its human enemies. We do not know how many more people this earth can provide for nor at what level of existence, but we do know there is a limit, and we are rapidly approaching it. We do not know how much wider the gap can grow between the rich and poor nations of the world, before all of humanity perishes in the battle of Armageddon. But we know there is a limit to how much suffering and oppression people will and can endure. We do not know the extent of the earth's nonrenewable natural resources, but we do know that the world is running out of gas. We do not know how much pollution this earth can absorb before man will forfeit his "dominion over the fish of the sea, and over the birds of the air, and over the cattle, and over all the earth, and over every creeping thing that creeps upon the earth" (Gen. 1:26). But there is a limit.

What is being driven home to us is the finitude of man and his environment. This is an awareness which has diminished with the decline of religious influence in modern culture. For religion has classically said that there is only One who is infinite; the world and all its creatures are finite. As every person can bear only so many burdens and then his back breaks, so the earth —like a vessel—has a limited carrying capacity. Kenneth Boulding has developed the metaphor of life on a spaceship.

> We have to visualize the earth as a small, rather crowded spaceship, destination unknown, in which man has to find a slender thread of a way of life in the midst of a continually repeated cycle of material transformations. In a spaceship, there can be no inputs or outputs. The water must circulate through the kidneys and the algae, the food likewise, the air likewise. . . . Up to now the human population has been small enough so that we have not had to regard the earth as a spaceship. We have been able to regard the atmosphere and the oceans and even the soil as an inexhaustible reservoir, from which we can draw at will and which we can pollute at will. There is handwriting on the wall, however. . . . Even now we may be doing irreversible damage to this precious little spaceship.[2]

False Axioms of Salvation

There is still an abundant optimism that if scientific technology has gotten the spaceship into trouble, it will fix whatever is wrong. Technology can save us! But can it really? The debate rages. Technological optimists believe that there are technical solutions to the problems that face us, and we will find them in time. Critics of technological salvation say that technology works only on the symptoms even while making things worse at the causal level. There are human dimensions—social, political and cultural—which have deep roots in the religious and moral sensibilities of people which make purely technological solutions seem superficial and even disastrous.

The authors of *The Limits to Growth* are all members of our technological culture. But they say, "We have found that technological optimism is the most common and the most dangerous reaction to our findings from the world model. Technology can relieve the symptoms of a problem without affecting the underlying causes. Faith in technology as the ultimate solution to all problems can thus divert our attention from the most fundamental problem—the problem of growth in a finite system —and prevent us from taking effective action to solve it." [3] On the other hand, it is folly to make technology the new demonology. Some of our problems—given the present stage of the world's development—will not be solved without technology, no matter how successful we become in reaching a desirable state of global equilibrium. Population growth will not be reduced without better contraceptive measures and pollution will not be eliminated without radically improved devices. Technology will play a part in better communications between nations and more effective sharing of all the goods we have to go around.

It would be especially cruel to demonize technology—the heart of our advanced industrialized society—when the nations of the Third World are struggling to achieve a higher standard of living through technological development. The ecological problem calls for a global solution, and that solution will inevitably embrace two steps: First, the United States and other advanced industrialized nations must sooner or later realize the folly of their growth mentality. For the sake of global justice they will be forced to decelerate, and to save themselves from the jaws of their own technological Frankenstein they will have to enter intentionally into a phase of de-development. The earth is simply too small for all the nations of the world to catch up to the rate of industrialization and productivity of the United States. Therefore, if global justice is to prevail as a future condition of international equilibrium, the United States will have to cut back to a reasonable standard of living. Secondly, the nations of the Third World will have to develop the concept of alternative technology. Technology yes, but not Western style, which only means destruction of the earth and death to its peoples.

Our Ethical Bankruptcy

If we formulate the conditions that seem essential to a viable and desirable future for mankind, we will be accused of speaking the language of utopian hope. For there is scant evidence from human history to arouse easy confidence that leaders and nations ever embark on a course that proceeds from other than narrow egoistic motives, that they will make the sacrifice of national sovereignty for the sake of world community, that they will abandon their competitive and conflictive modes of behavior. If civilization is to survive, we must postulate the arrival of new and unprecedented changes in value structure, attitudinal make-up, educational praxis, and life style. We simply cannot get to a good future for mankind the way we are going now. Our cultural cupboards are bare, our ethical reserves are bankrupt. Our past has not prepared us for the new imperatives that are calculated to meet the magnitude of our ecological problem.

There are fundamentally two courses that lie before us. Either we continue the present course of disintegrating development, moving from this decade of growing tensions in the world system to the coming decades of desperation and catastrophe, eating our way into the future from hand to mouth, or, we proclaim the need for basically new values, new social systems, new political structures, in short, a new birth of consciousness. This new consciousness will be future-oriented, giving rise to new models, new symbols, new songs, new rituals, new myths, a new vision of the future and a conversion of will to actualize it. I am not saying these new things will necessarily come, only that the alternative is to tinker with the old system which is speedily ushering in the apocalypse of annihilation.

Ethicists are the middle-men between technologists and theologians. Traditionally, ethical reflection has been oriented to the past, dealing with such topics as the orders of life going back to creation or with the unchanging structures of natural law. Ethics lifted up the values of obedience to authority and duty to the normative traditions that derive from the past. I do not believe that the ethical wisdom of the past is now obsolete and meaningless with respect to the personal and the interpersonal spheres of behavior. But I do believe that our traditional ethic tends to lean backwards to the past, and therefore becomes speechless and helpless in coping with the actions which bear heavily on the destiny of the coming generations.

The attempt of some contemporary ethicists to free ethics from this bondage to past norms and principles in favor of a "situation ethics" is a total failure with respect to the ecological problem. We cannot wait until we get into the situation of crisis and decision, and then intuit the right thing to do. For then it will be too late; our society will have reached the point of no return. If an engine is racing toward an abyss, there comes a time when it's pointless to apply the brakes. An ethics of the future looks ahead for its clues as to what to do now. It studies the future to see what in the present is basically destroying the prospects of a just and fulfilling future for all people. The ethical problem is no longer to develop standards of behavior for past situations. They may never recur. The ethical question is not merely, "Have I done what is right?" Rather, it is this, "Do I (or we) have the right to do such and such?" And the answer to that question is not whether it conforms to the moral standards of the past, but instead whether it is a means of bringing promise for the future. This is an ethic of promise—a prospective ethic!

What makes a future-oriented ethic imperative today is the role that prognosis and planning play in modern society. Ethical reflection must take into account all the facts and then propose a decision. Part of these facts are still future; they are things that have not yet happened but certainly will if the present trends continue. If ethical reflection is not effectually present where political and technological powers are planning our future, then it will enter as an irrelevant *post mortem*. The ethicists of the future must carry a vision of the *humanum,* of the essential humanity of man, into the forums of planning and decision-making. They may not leave the planning of the future to technological types. These may be giants in stature when it comes to technical means, but moral pygmies on issues of human concern. Jacques Ellul is correct when he says of Einstein: "It is clear that Einstein, extraordinary mathematical genius that he was, was no Pascal; he knew nothing of political or human reality, or, in fact, anything at all outside his mathematical reach. The banality of Einstein's remarks in matters outside his specialty is as astonishing as his genius within it." [4]

Imagineering the Future

I have been asserting that the ecological problem demands a
new ethical stance towards man's natural environment—a future-
oriented ethic that is determined by a vision of the essential
humanity of man and his natural brotherhood with the world
of nature. It won't work to give humanists the past, politicians
the present and technocrats the future to engineer it to death.
In addition to these engineers of the future, we need an army
of imaginers of a new world. But where will the images of a more
human future and a new earth come from?

Willy-nilly some sets of values and interests are being served
by any group which holds the power of the future in their hands.
The dominant values and interests of the major power blocs in
the world today are leading, as we have said, to despair, disaster
and death to all that lives and breathes on this planet. People
who care about the future of man and this earth must find ways
to replace those values and interests with new ones. They must
function with alternative models of the future. These will necessarily have visionary character, for no such models can be trans-
ferred from past experiences and precedents. When the authors
of *The Limits to Growth* have completed their analysis of the
world as it approaches the ultimate limits of a finite system,
they hold out a few straws of hope. But just at this point they
cease to be hard-headed technological realists and become human
beings animated by extraordinary hope. The realistic consequence of their analysis would be anxiety and despair. But they
transcend their own realism, and begin to postulate new steps
for humanity, the possibility of creating a "totally new form of
human society." [5] There are only two missing ingredients: one
is a meaningful goal that can guide humanity to an equilibrium
society that this earth can support, and another is a commitment
of will to achieve that goal. But that is utopian language, for
such a goal and such a will are really new things. They are certainly not in line with the drives and tendencies that people
and nations exhibit today.

"None of our wise men ever pose the question of the end of
all their marvels," [6] says Jacques Ellul. The survival of mankind
under more fulfilling conditions of life for all will assuredly call
for a new breed of wise men. There is no guarantee that humanity will not go the way of the dodo and the dinosaur. Naturally,

as a human being I am prejudiced, but I think mankind is worth saving. We have termites in the foundations of our house. We believe our house is worth saving, so we go after the termites. And the house will stand as a comfortable place to live. So it is with the earth. It is a nice place to live. But getting rid of the termites won't be easy, because people are the termites. The ecology movement has coined the saying that people plus pollution means *populution*. And that is why we will need wise men, experts in the science of the *humanum,* in the days to come.

While rummaging through a bookstore, I ran across a new book entitled, *This Endangered Planet, Prospects and Proposals for Human Survival,* by Richard A. Falk. I hope it will be a much read and much discussed book. He writes one paragraph which states precisely what I am proposing: "There are several steps that need to be taken: first, we need to understand the inability of the sovereign state to resolve the endangered-planet crisis; second, we need a model of world order that provides a positive vision of the future and is able to resolve this crisis; third, we need a strategy that will transform human attitudes and institutions so as to make it politically possible to bring a new system of world order into being; fourth, we need specific programs to initiate the process, as with learning to walk—we need to learn to walk into the future." [7]

We need to work out a whole new world view which is shaped by the horizon of the future, of a noble, beautiful, harmonious, human and planetary future. Our private and individual futures cannot go their own way *laissez-faire*. We adopt the ecological notion that the destiny of each individual must be seen as linked to the future of the total system. The salvation of mankind is not a free-for-all, each one grabbing what he can out of the commons that exists for all alike.

A future-oriented ethic that can help to humanize technology cannot live from itself. It must be hinged to a holistic image of the future that pulls humanity out of the ditch onto a high road. Such a picture of the future may release a new spurt of the human spirit, alluring and activating it to seek goals and pursue actions that previously seemed incredible. There is a very close link between images of the future and ethics. Ethics deal with the realm of what ought to be; our picture of the future can mirror what ought to be and give shape to it in a way that contrasts radically with the actual present. Our dominant habits of thought in the West have been crippling this mental capacity to visualize a different future. But when we lose our power to envision a future alternative to the extant present, we have lost our freedom, and thereby our dignity and our humanity. We have become machine-like robots. The widespread despair in our time, manifest in the use of mind-blowing drugs, nerve-jarring music, high rates of killing speed, world-escaping religion, and fascination for the occult, can be explained by the loss of faith in the power of the future to bring something different than the present holds.

The Educational Task

The development of an ecological humanism that is world-wide will require a rebirth of images of the future that are still alive—although latent—in the religious culture of the world. There are rich deposits of such culturally significant images in the classical period of Greece and Rome, in the Scriptures of Israel and primitive Christianity. These futuristic images of man in the world produced the utopias of the Renaissance; they gave birth to the impulses of freedom in the Reformation, the drive to emancipated reason in the Enlightenment, the revolution to justice in modern socialism, the belief in scientific progress in the nineteenth century, and finally the hope for the unity of mankind in the twentieth century ecumenical movement. These images of the future have worked like a flying wedge on the frontiers of time, clearing the way for the troops in history, inspiring their courage and arousing their hope. These images of hope have kept the spirit of men and women alive with fiery enthusiasm. When the images die or become contracted to the pragmatics of the present moment, we are at the begining of the end of a civilization. A culture with no driving image of the future has come to the end of its history; it has lost its lever of movement and progress.

If the history of culture is the history of its images of the future, as Frederick Polak says,[8] the most urgent challenge facing mankind today is the creation and renewal of a living faith in the realm of the future beckoning on the world's horizon. We are viewing the crisis of our culture—the eco-crisis—as a spiritual problem beyond the scope of technological salvation. People will not care for a future they do not believe in. Considering the ecological dimension of the problem of the future, we are seemingly speaking of a faith which can move mountains.

William Pollard, well-known scientist and author, says that this faith will probably not be forthcoming short of a catastrophe of unspeakable tragedy. "We can only foresee social paroxysms of an intensity greater than we have so far known. The problems are so varied and so vast and the means for their solution so far beyond the resources of the scientific and technological know-how on which we have relied that there is simply not time to avoid the impending catastrophe. We stand, therefore, on the threshold of a time of judgment more severe, undoubtedly, than any that mankind has ever faced before in history." [9] And yet he chooses to believe that on the other side of judgment there is hope for man and the earth. Man will come to appreciate the beauty and the holiness of the earth, to woo and to love it, luring it into ever more creative achievements. However, "to do this it is first necessary for man widely and generally to recover his lost sense of transcendent reality." [10]

I would rather make the impending catastrophe conditional. It is coming *unless* man ceases the rape of the earth. The future is still open; there is still time to reverse the process. That is the educational task that faces us. But where will a people be found who already begin to live the life of a wholesome future under the conditions of the present? The positive aspects of the future must make openings in the present for people to experience. Education must become anticipatory; activity must be expectational. Thinking and acting must have a thrust to the future, to break the bad habits we have learned from the past. The study of history is an essential component of a whole curriculum. But our children, like we ourselves, are only getting half an education, because we do not teach them to think and live from the future back to the present, from the whole to the parts, from the end-state to all the steps leading to it. The maps of our world are still flat; we don't see the whole in all its multi-dimensional complexity. Alvin Toffler writes: "When millions share this passion about the future we shall have a society far better equipped to meet the impact of change. To create such curiosity and awareness is a cardinal task of education. To create an education that will create this curiosity is the third, and perhaps central, mission of the super-industrial revolution in the schools. Education must shift into the future tense." [11]

We need a future-conscious community of committed people who care for the future and will make it their life mission to infiltrate all other communities with the good and bad news about the future. They must come from the ranks of scientists and technologists, politicians and economists, but also poets and priests. They will be united by a common vision of the future in which technology becomes domesticated, strictly a tool applied to worthy human ends. Not the question, "What can we do?" but rather, "What ought we to do?" will define our priorities. But this ethical question of what is right depends radically on a vision of the good. Since we can have no photographic pictures of what is good, for the good that we seek is yet to come, we hold our pictures of the good as images of the future. They have a kind of double exposure; they mirror the present in its needs and lacks and they hold up a future in its possible glory and grandeur, and in this double way they work retroactively, as it were, in shaping the present values and decisions of people.

One of the cultural imperatives which the ecological crisis lays upon us is the overcoming of the artificial divorce between religion and science. Such a divorce is a luxury our culture can no longer afford. We all live in one world and breathe the same air. The future of science and technology cannot be discussed apart from the values and goals which command the interests and loyalties of the masses of people. No one can discuss for long the ecological crisis before complex ethical issues are raised.

Christianity entered the world with an eschatological vision of the future of the world. It is still the dominant religion in the West. The question it faces is whether its belief in the future has any relevance to the universal dialog concerning a more human future of all mankind. It is a common failing of religious people to link their hopes to a purely other-worldly future or to an inner-personal salvation. And that is precisely why many people who deal with the hard decisions that bear on the technological and social future of mankind expect little help from the church and its religious and ethical beliefs. Hopefully the renewal of the Christian vision of the eschatological future of man and his world and the qualities of its promises and hopes will commingle with the models of the future which are now being constructed by an elite corps of futurologists in every country. The role of a compassionate religion is simply to keep the spotlight on the human face of man in every discussion, in every experiment, in every scheme that futurologists devise, especially the human face of those who are poor, powerless and futureless, so that the least of all our fellow beings may be liberated for a fulfilling life on earth. The ethical criterion that should be applied in every contribution to technological progress is: what does it imply for the future of man and his environment? The human factor must always provide the normative element in discussing the wonders of technology and our ecological future. This homocentric concern is the point at which ecology and ethics meet.

As scientists, technologists, statesmen, industrialists, ethicists and theologians become pressed to take up this theme of caring for the future on a universal scale, they will quickly experience the frustration of using futuristic language in different frames of reference. In scientific and technological futurology, the future is the exemplification of trends extrapolated forward from the present. In a future-oriented ethic the future attains a dual meaning; it is like a rear-view mirror, giving us a view of past and present realities from a futurist point of reference, and at the same time like a spotlight pointing ahead showing the way we ought to go. The decisive element in ethical language is the dimension of oughtness, for that gives expression to the self-transcending dynamic essential to the humanity of man. We have not been speaking of the future in a strictly theological sense in this chapter. Theology speaks of the ultimate future of man and of the world. It speaks of God as the power of the future of man and of the world. It speaks of God as the power of the future that confronts every present, placing it under judgment and also mediating new possibilities. The future of futurology and the future of theology are not therefore completely unattached and unrelated. There is a point of contact, namely, in identifying the ground and source of the new which must intervene if the future of man and the earth is to enjoy a quality leap beyond the confines of the present, if the future is to be something more than a quantitative prolongation of the past and the present, if there is to be a real future that matches the promises we bear as vessels of hope. It is hope that teaches us about the other dimension of the future, that makes us restless until we break out of the one-dimensionalism that today threatens to destroy the humanity of man and the world that houses him.

NOTES

Chapter One

1. Wolfhart Pannenberg, "Can Christianity Do Without An Eschatology?" *The Christian Hope* (London: S.P.C.K., 1970), pp. 29-30.
2. Wolfhart Pannenberg, *Theology and the Kingdom of God* (The Westminster Press, 1969), p. 53.
3. Wolfhart Pannenberg, *Jesus—God and Man* (The Westminster Press, 1968), pp. 19-37, 53-107.
4. Karl Jaspers, *Philosophical Faith and Revelation* (London: Collins, 1967), p. 314.
5. Jürgen Moltmann, *Theology of Hope* (Harper & Row, 1967), p. 64.
6. Robert W. Jenson, *The Knowledge of Things Hoped For* (Oxford University Press, 1969).
7. The statement is by Ernest Gellner but quoted by Ved Mehta, *Fly and the Fly-Bottle* (Penguin Books, 1965), p. 39.
8. Herbert Marcuse, *One-Dimensional Man* (London: Routledge & Kegan Paul, Ltd., 1964), p. 175.
9. *Ibid.*, p. 173, n. 2.
10. See Ernest Gellner, *Words and Things* (Boston: Beacone Press, 1959).
11. Teilhard de Chardin, *Letters from a Traveller* (Harper & Row, 1962), p. 21.
12. Quoted in Ernst Benz, *Evolution and Christian Hope* (Doubleday & Company, 1966), p. 209.
13. Teilhard de Chardin, *The Future of Man* (Harper & Row, 1964), p. 137.
14. Teilhard de Chardin, *The Vision of the Past* (Harper & Row, 1966), p. 187.
15. *Ibid.*, p. 188.
16. *Ibid.*, p. 199.
17. Teilhard de Chardin, *The Future of Man*, p. 61.
18. *Ibid.*, p. 70.
19. Teilhard de Chardin, *The Vision of the Past*, p. 159.
20. Wolfhart Pannenberg, *The Idea of God and Human Freedom* (The Westminster Press, 1973), p. 198.
21. *Ibid.*, p. 199.
22. See Wolfhart Pannenberg, "Future and Unity," *Hope and the Future of Man*, edited by Ewert Cousins (Fortress Press, 1972), pp. 60-77.
23. Bernard Lonergan, *Method in Theology* (Herder & Herder, 1972), p. 163.

Chapter Two

1. Bernard Lonergan, *Method in Theology* (Herder & Herder, 1972).
2. Bernard Lonergan, *Insight, A Study of Human Understanding* (Longmans, Green and Co., Ltd., 1957).
3. Charles Davis, "Lonergan and the Teaching Church," *Foundations of Theology*, edited by Philip McShane (Dublin: Gill and Macmillan, 1971), p. 62.
4. Lonergan, *Insight*, xviii-xxiii, xxviii.
5. See Schubert Ogden, "Lonergan and the Subjectivist Principle," *Language, Truth and Meaning*, edited by Philip McShane (Dublin: Gill and Macmillan, 1973).
6. Lonergan, *Insight*, xii.
7. *Ibid.*, xxviii.
8. *Ibid.*, p. 73.
9. *Ibid.*, p. 396.
10. See Robert W. Jenson, *The Knowledge of Things Hoped* (Oxford University Press, 1969).
11. Lonergan, *Insight*, pp. 53 ff.
12. *Ibid.*, ix.
13. Lonergan, *Method in Theology*, p. 130.
14. Ernst Bloch, *Das Prinzip Hoffnung* (Suhrkamp Verlag, 1959), Vol. I, p. 5.
15. Lonergan, *Insight*, p. 660.
16. Ernst Bloch, *Das Prinzip Hoffnung*, Vol. III, p. 1628.
17. Wolfhart Pannenberg, *Basic Questions in Theology* (Fortress Press, 1971), Vol. II, pp. 1-27.
18. Lonergan, *Insight*, p. 447 f.
19. Lonergan, *Method in Theology*, p. 137.
20. Pannenberg, *Basic Questions in Theology*, Vol. I, pp. 96-136.

Chapter Three

1. William Dilthey, *Pattern and Meaning in History*, selections from the *Gesammelte Schriften*, Vol. VII, edited by H. P. Rickman (Harper & Row, 1961), p. 106. This is the fuller statement: "The category of meaning designates the relation, rooted in life itself, of parts to the whole . . . the single moment derives its meaning from its connection with the whole, from the relation between future and past, between the individual and mankind."
2. Wolfhart Pannenberg, *Basic Questions in Theology* (Fortress Press, 1970), p. 69.

Chapter Four

1. Quoted by Walter Kaufmann, "Existentialism and Death," in *The Meaning of Death*, edited by Herman Feifel (New York: McGraw-Hill Book Company, 1959), p. 48
2. Paul Ricoeur, *Freedom and Nature: The Voluntary and the Involuntary* (Northwestern University Press, 1966), p. 462.
3. Quoted by Walter Kaufmann, "Existentialism and Death," *op. cit.*, p. 48.
4. *Plato, Selections*, edited by Raphael Demos (New York: Charles Scribner's Sons, 1927), p. 32.
5. Walter Kaufmann, *op. cit.*, p. 61.
6. *Ibid.*, p. 62.

Chapter Five

1. Mark Gibbs and T. Ralph Morton, *God's Frozen People* (The Westminster Press, 1964), p. 16.
2. This is to be found in Luther's fourteenth proposal for reform in his appeal *To the Christian Nobility.*
3. Quoted from Heinz Brunotte, *Das Geistliche Amt bei Luther* (Berlin, 1959), p. 26.

Chapter Six

1. Harper & Row, 1972.
2. Article XXVIII.
3. J. D. Benoit, *Liturgical Renewal* (SCM Press, 1958), p. 104.
4. Fortress Press, 1973.
5. John A. T. Robinson, *Liturgy Coming to Life* (A. R. Mowbray & Co., 1969), p. 10.
6. John A. T. Robinson, *On Being the Church in the World* (SCM Press, 1960), p. 68.
7. H. Richard Niebuhr, *The Purpose of the Church and Its Ministry* (Harper & Row, 1956), p. 81.

Chapter Seven

1. James M. Gustafson, *Christian Ethics and the Community* (Philadelphia: United Church Press, 1971), p. 23.
2. This generalization may be subject to some qualification. A brief discussion of eschatology and ethics in J. Moltmann's *Theology of Hope* appears in Professor Gene Outka's recent book, *Agape, An Ethical Analysis* (Yale University Press, 1972), pp. 178-181.
3. Helmut Thielicke, *Theological Ethics*, Vol. I (Philadelphia: Fortress Press, 1966), p. 47.
4. Paul Ramsey, *Basic Christian Ethics* (New York: Charles Scribner's Sons, 1951), p. 41.
5. Reinhold Niebuhr, *An Interpretation of Christian Ethics* (New York: Harper & Bros., 1935), p. 59.
6. *Ibid.*, p. 43.
7. Quoted in Richard Neuhaus' introduction to *Theology and the Kingdom of God*, by Wolfhart Pannenberg (Philadelphia: The Westminster Press, 1969), p. 32.
8. T. W. Manson, *Ethics and the Gospel* (New York: Charles Scribner's Sons, 1960), p. 65.
9. In the "Introduction" by Richard H. Hiers and D. Larrimore Holland of Johannes Weiss's book, *Jesus' Proclamation of the Kingdom of God* (Philadelphia: Fortress Press, 1971), p. 25.
10. Cf., Richard Hiers, *Jesus and Ethics* (Philadelphia: The Westminster Press, 1968); also, Richard Hiers, *The Kingdom of God in the Synoptic Tradition* (Gainesville, Fla.: The University of Florida Press, 1970).
11. Johannes Weiss, *op. cit.*, p. 114.
12. Günter Klein, "The Biblical Understanding of 'The Kingdom of God'," *Interpretation* (October 1972), Vol. XXV, No. 4, p. 399.
13. Cf. Wolfhart Pannenberg, "The Kingdom of God and the Foundation of Ethics," in *Theology and the Kingdom of God*, op. cit., pp. 102-126.

Notes

14. Cf. William K. Frankena, *Ethics* (Englewood Cliffs, N.J.: Prentice-Hall, Inc., 1963); also, William K. Frankena, "Love and Principle in Christian Ethics," in *Faith anod Philosophy*, edited by Alvin Plantinga (Grand Rapids, Mich.: Wm. B. Eerdmans, 1964).
15. William K. Frankena, *Ethics, op. cit.*, p. 43.
16. Paul Ramsey, *Deeds and Rules in Christian Ethics* (New York: Charles Scribner's Sons, 1967), pp. 108, 109.
17. H. Richard Niebuhr, *The Responsible Self* (New York: Harper & Row, 1963).
18. Cf. William A. Johnson's study of Nygren's thought, *On Religion: A Study of Theological Method in Schleiermacher and Nygren* (Leiden, Neth.: Brill, 1964).
19. William K. Frankena, *Ethics, op. cit.*, pp. 43 ff.
20. Paul Lehmann, *Ethics in a Christian Context* (New York: Harper & Row, 1963), p. 45.
21. It was Karl Barth, after all, who stated in his *Commentary on the Epistle to the Romans*, "Christianity that is not entirely and altogether eschatology has entirely and altogether nothing to do with Christ" (Oxford University Press, 1963), p. 314.
22. Paul Tillich, *Systematic Theology*, Vol. III (Chicago: The University of Chicago Press, 1963), pp. 358-359.
23. Dorothee Sölle, *Beyond Mere Obedience*, trans. by Lawrence W. Denef (Minneapolis, Minn.: Augsburg Publishing House, 1970), especially chapter 2.

Chapter Eight

1. Otto Feinstein, ed., *Ethnic Groups in the City* (D. C. Heath and Company, 1971), p. 193.
2. Richard Rubenstein, *After Auschwitz: Essays in Contemporary Judaism* (The Bobbs-Merrill Company, 1966), p. 70.
3. On religious socialism, see Paul Tillich's essays, "Religious Socialism" and "Basic Principles of Religious Socialism" in *Political Expectation*, edited by James Luther Adams (Harper & Row, 1971).

Chapter Nine

1. Quoted in Nicholas Lobkowicz, *Theory and Practice: History of a Concept from Aristotle to Marx* (University of Notre Dame Press, 1967), p. 121.
2. *Ibid.*
3. *Ibid.*, p. 122.
4. Gustavo Gutierrez, *A Theology of Liberation* (Orbis Books, 1973), pp. 6-15.
5. Richard Bernstein, *Praxis and Action* (University of Pennsylvania Press, 1971), xi.
6. N. Lobkowicz, *op. cit.*, p. 274.
7. Jürgen Moltmann, *Religion, Revolution and the Future* (Charles Scribner's Sons, 1969), p. 138.
8. Johannes B. Metz, *Theology of the World* (Herder & Herder, 1969), p. 112.
9. G. Gutierrez, *op. cit.*, p. 14.
10. *Ibid.*, p. 15.
11. Friedrich-Wilhelm Marquardt, *Theologie und Sozialismus. Das Beispiel Karl Barths* (Chr. Kaiser Verlag, 1972), p. 321.

12. *Ibid.*
13. Cf. especially an unpublished study document by Paul Tillich, in the Tillich archives at Harvard Divinity School, entitled "The Christian and the Marxist View of Man," which apparently served as the basis for a number of his briefer writings dealing with Marxism. This document was prepared for the research department of the "Universal Christian Council for Life and Work," bearing the date, December, 1935.
14. N. Lobkowicz, *op. cit.*, p. 159.
15. *Ibid.*, p. 412.
16. Quoted by Jürgen Habermas, *Knowledge and Human Interests* (Beacon Press, 1971), p. 301.
17. Paulo Freire, *Pedagogy of the Oppressed* (Herder & Herder, 1970).
18. René Dubos, *Man Adapting* (Yale University Press, 1965), p. 425.

Chapter Twelve

1. Donella H. Meadows, Dennis L. Meadows, Jørgen Randers, William W. Behrens III, *The Limits to Growth* (Universe Books, 1972).
2. Kenneth E. Boulding, *Human Values on the Spaceship Earth* (New York: National Council of Churches, 1966), p. 6.
3. *The Limits to Growth, op. cit.*, p. 159.
4. Jacques Ellul, *The Technological Society* (Alfred A. Knopf, Inc., 1964), p. 435.
5. *The Limits to Growth, op. cit.*, p. 188.
6. Jacques Ellul, *The Technological Society, op. cit.*, p. 436.
7. Richard A. Falk, *This Endangered Planet* (Random House, Inc., 1972), p. 15.
8. Frederick Polak, *The Image of the Future* (Oceana Publications, 1961), Vol. II, p. 115.
9. William Pollard, "The Uniqueness of the Earth," *Earth Might Be Fair* (Prentice-Hall, Inc., 1972), p. 96.
10. *Ibid.*, p. 97.
11. Alvin Toffler, *Future Shock* (Random House, Inc., 1970), p. 427.